Ecommerce
Evolved

By
Tanner Larsson

Printed in the United States of America

First Printing 2016

ISBN-13: 978-1534619340
ISBN-10: 1534619348

Cover Design by:
Fiaz Ahmed Irfan
Islamabad - Pakistan

Interior Design by:
BookClaw.com

Illustrations by:
Carla Giampapa
Bloomicon/Shutterstock.com

10580 N. McCarran Blvd, #115-329
Reno, NV 89503-2059
www.BuildGrowScale.com

Table of Contents

DEDICATION xv

INTRODUCTION 1

    Why I Wrote This Book 4

    Why This Book Is Different 5

    Four Distinctions That Set This Book Apart 7

        1. The Vital Few 7

        2. Zero Theory 7

        3. Evergreen Training 8

        4. Systematic Immersion 8

THE 12 CORE PRINCIPLES OF ECOMMERCE 11

    1. Your Business is Not Unique 12

    2. Your Business is Marketing 14

    3. Brand Centric, Not Product Centric 15

    4. You Must Control the Order Process 15

    5. Don't Compete on Price 18

    6. Don't Be Walmart. Niche Down. 20

    7. No Such Thing as Free Traffic 22

    8. Business Costs Money 24

    9. If You're Not Mobile, You're Out 25

10. The One Who Can Spend the Most to Acquire a Customer Wins 26

11. Sell in Multiple Channels 28

12. There Are Only Three Ways to Grow a Business 30

Conclusion.. 32

PART I:Evolved Strategy 35

CHAPTER 1: Funnel-Based Ecommerce 39

The Two Worlds of Ecommerce....................................... 40

Why Funnel-Based Ecommerce is So Effective.............. 41

The Proof Is in the Numbers 42

The Buyer's High 43

Pieces of a Sales Funnel 44

Front End... 45

Order Bump 45

Upsell... 47

Downsell 49

Recurring Income Offer (RIC Offer)........................... 51

Products.. 51

The Two Types of Ecom Funnels.................................... 52

The Stand-Alone Funnel... 53

The Upsell Funnel Path 54

Default Upsell Funnel Paths 56

Product-Specific Upsell Funnel Paths 56

Behavior-Based Upsell Funnel Paths........................... 57

Incorporating Sales Funnels into Your Business.............. 58

What About My Store? 59

Conclusion.. 60

Chapter 1 Summary 61

CHAPTER 2: Recurring Income Core 63

The Power of Recurring Income 64

Recurring Income as the Focal Point of Your Business .. 65

Predictable Income.... *67*

Compound Growth Effect *69*

Types, Styles, and Frequencies of Recurring Income
Cores 70

Types of Recurring Income Cores.................................... 70

Consumable Subscriptions.... *71*

Subscription Box *71*

Digital... *72*

Newsletters (Physical or Digital) *73*

Buyer's Clubs *74*

Associations... *74*

Micro Continuity *75*

Choosing RIC Types... *76*

Styles of Recurring Income Core....................................... 77

Subscription.. *78*

Membership... *78*

Hybrid *79*

Frequencies.. 79

Adding a Recurring Income Core to Your Business 80

Technology... 81

Selling Your RIC 81

Upsells *82*

Trials *82*

Multiple Continuity Streams 83

Retention Management 84

The 10x Rule 85

Retention Metrics 86

1. Churn Rate (CR)... *86*

   2. Customer Count Retention (CCR).......................... *86*

   3. Average Subscription Revenue Per Customer (ASRC)....... *87*

Drop-Off Points.. 88

Make Canceling Simple, But Not Painless 92

Conclusion.. 93

Chapter 2 Summary 94

CHAPTER 3: Think Before You Sell **95**

Product Pricing: It's All About the Margin 96

The 3X Rule.. 100

   What If the Product You Love Doesn't Meet the 3x Rule?... *102*

Sell Your Own Products 103

Don't Sell Sony... 103

Product Selection and Manufacturer Selection Criteria.. 105

   Product Selection.. *105*

   Manufacturer Criteria:.. *108*

Private Label 109

Original Equipment Manufacturing (OEM) 111

   Is Your Product Viable? *114*

Outside the Box... 115

   Print On Demand.. *116*

   Crowdfunding.. *117*

   Crowdsourcing *117*

   Don't Forget About Digital Products........................... *119*

Product Fulfillment.. 121

   Arbitrage.. *121*

   Drop Ship *123*

   Third-Party Fulfillment *124*

   In-House Fulfillment *126*

Conclusion.. 128

Chapter 3 Summary 129

CHAPTER 4: Conversion Tricks, Sales Boosts, and
Profit Maximizers **131**

Conversion Tricks 132

Retargeting... 132

How to Retarget *134*

Product Reviews... 135

Landing Pages 137

Components of a Landing Page........................... 138

Unique Mobile Checkout..................................... 141

Sales Boosts.. 142

Loss Leaders... 143

Tripwires... 144

Flash Sales 145

The Phone Doesn't Bite....................................... 145

Profit Maximizers 147

Free Shipping 147

Shipping and Handling as a Profit Center 149

Ride-Alongs... 150

Conclusion.. 152

Chapter 4 Summary 153

PART II:Evolved Intelligence **155**

CHAPTER 5: Your Target Market **159**

Demographics... 161

Customer Demographics...................................... *162*

Tools for Finding Audience Data 164

Facebook Insights *165*

Facebook Audience Insights *165*

TowerData *166*

Twitter Analytics.. *167*

Alexa *167*

Google Analytics.. *168*

Survey *168*

Social and Behavior Data 168

Social and Behavioral Data *169*

Tools for Finding Social and Behavioral Data............... 170

Facebook... *170*

Niche Magazines.. *171*

Google *171*

SimilarWeb.. *172*

Your Customer Avatar 172

1. Demographics 174

2. The Seven Emotional Questions....................... 174

The Seven Emotional Questions............................... *175*

3. The Ten Behavioral Questions *175*

4. Create a Background Story.................................. *177*

Example of a Customer Avatar................................ *177*

Can You Have More Than One Customer Avatar?............. *179*

Conclusion.. 180

Chapter 5 Summary 181

CHAPTER 6: Your Competition...............................**183**

Find Your Biggest Competitors 184

How to Find Your Competitors *185*

1. Google... *185*

2. SEMrush *186*

3. Alexa *187*

The Three Steps to Find Your Competition................ *188*

Document How Each Competitor Operates.................. 188

Competitor Research Checklist................................. 190

Reverse-Engineer Your Competition.............................192

    1. SEMrush...*193*

    2. BuzzSumo *194*

    3. WhatRunsWhere *194*

    4. SimilarWeb...*195*

    5. Ghostery...*196*

Funnel Hack...197

    How to Execute a Funnel Hack..........................*198*

Conclusion..199

Chapter 6 Summary 200

CHAPTER 7: Exploit Your Data **201**

Internal Data Patterns and Analysis 203

Basket Analysis 203

Sales Forecasting...205

Inventory Forecasting..208

Channel Analysis 209

    Device Used for Purchase *211*

Customer Analysis...212

    Repeat Customers, Continuity Buyers, and Whales..............*212*

    Regional Affinity *213*

    Demographics *214*

    Payment Preference................................*214*

    Shipping Preference *214*

Find Your Low-Hanging Fruit............................215

Profile Your Buyer's List.....................................215

    Facebook Audience Insights *216*

    TowerData *216*

Curated Facebook Audiences..............................217

    Facebook Custom Audiences....................*217*

    Possible Facebook Custom Audiences.......................*219*

Facebook Lookalike Audiences 219

Facebook Pixel 220

Honeypot Traffic 220

Referral Traffic 221

Data-Driven Promotions 221

Conclusion 222

Chapter 7 Summary 223

PART III: Evolved Marketing **225**

CHAPTER 8: Advertising Channels **227**

Core Ecommerce Marketing Channels 229

Traffic You Own 230

Traffic You Own 230

Traffic You Control 231

Paid Advertisement 231

Affiliates 232

Paid Traffic Sources 233

Traffic You Don't Control 233

Marketplaces 234

Organic or Unpaid Advertisement 235

Social Media 236

Comparison Shopping Engine (CSE) 236

Unpaid Traffic Sources 237

Tips for Channel Success 238

Avoid Channel Dependence 238

Take it Slow 240

Breach Consumer Ecosystems 240

Traffic Temperature 241

Cold Traffic 242

Warm Traffic 243

Hot Traffic 243

Conclusion.. 245

Chapter 8 Summary 245

CHAPTER 9: Front-End Marketing...........................247

Why Traffic Is Not Your Problem 248

Combating Your Bounce and Abandonment Rates 250

Active Advertising.. 251

Customer Acquisition 252

Prospect Acquisition.. 253

A New World of Online Promotion 254

Campaigns and Content... 255
    Stumble Upon *257*
    Reddit *257*
    Twitter *258*
    Outbrain *258*
    Owned Media (Traffic You Own)................................. *258*

Retargeting... 259

Leveraging Traffic with Retargeting 259
    1. Cart Abandonment Promotion *261*
    2. Specific Product Promotion...................................... *262*
    3. List-Building Promotion *263*

Email Marketing.. 263

Email Away 264

Creating the Content.. 266

Always Track Your Emails 267

Dealing with Unsubscribes 268

Types of Email Campaigns 268
    The Indoctrination Campaign *269*
    Specifics *270*

The Welcome Email.. 271

The Core Offer Campaign... 272

Specifics.. 273

Tips for Featuring Different Products in Your Core Offer
Campaign.. 274

Bucket Promotions... 274

Default Promotion Vault 276

Types of Default Promotions... 277

1. Holiday-Based Promotions....................................... 278

2. Commercial Date Promotions 278

3. Brand-Related Promotions...................................... 278

4. Charity or Cause Promotion 279

5. Niche-specific Commemorative Day Promotions............... 279

Building Your Promotional Calendar............................... 279

Conclusion.. 281

Chapter 9 Summary 282

CHAPTER 10: Back-End Marketing 283

Customer Life Cycle 286

The Four Phases Of A Customer's Life Cycle................. 287

Granular Segmentation.. 288

Back-End Active Advertising...................................... 291

Repeat Purchases: The Focus of Back-End Active
Advertising 293

Back-End Retargeting Promotions............................... 294

Core Retargeting Promotions for Existing Customers... 294

1. Dynamic Product Ads... 294

2. Customer Reactivation.. 295

3. Active Advertising Support....................................... 296

Email Marketing on the Back End 296

Four Types of Campaigns 296
   1. New Customer Campaign.. 297
   2. Targeted Offer Campaigns 298
   3. VIP Campaigns... 299
   4. Win-Back Campaign 300
   Defection Times 300
   Techniques for Winning Back Customers 301
   Invest in Your Campaigns 303

Ignored Email Real Estate 303
   Receipt Email.. 303
   Shipping Notification or Tracking Link Email.................... 304

Conclusion.. 305

Chapter 10 Summary 306

FINAL THOUGHTS **307**

Quick Win Philosophy 307

Jump to The Front of the Line 308

ABOUT THE AUTHOR **311**

DEDICATION

To my mom, for never letting me settle and
always pushing me to succeed.

To my dad, for showing me early on that
being an entrepreneur was possible.

To my sister, for reminding me to live life on
my own terms and for leading by example.

To my wife Tabitha, for putting up with my
crazy ideas, allowing me to chase my dreams,
and always reminding me of my true worth.

And to my kids, Peyton and Paxton. You are
my *why* and you remind me every day what life
is all about.

INTRODUCTION

Hey, my name is Tanner Larsson and I am a self-admitted serial entrepreneur. I have started, co-founded, built, sold, scaled, bankrupted, and/or succeeded with over two dozen different companies in my career.

I have personally produced millions of dollars in revenue for my own ecom companies and over $75 million in revenue for companies I've partnered with, advised, or consulted for. Through this, I have experienced the myriad pendulum swings ecom businesses go through during their life cycle.

Going backward a bit, by profession I guess you could say that I am a window cleaner since that was the only "real" job I held before moving into the business world (ironically, by starting my own window-cleaning business). I tell you all of this to help you understand who I am and why I am writing this book.

I started selling physical products online back in 2001, when eBay first started growing. At the time I was still cultivating my offline business, but the entrepreneur in me couldn't resist the allure of selling things online. I immediately fell in love with it, and with the idea of being able to reach people all over the world.

I dove in headfirst and within a few months I had become a Power Seller on eBay, selling hundreds of products a day. It was at that point that I realized that my online business OWNED me and that I hated my life. My house had turned into a warehouse full of products and packing materials. Even worse, because in 2001 automation technology that we take for granted today either hadn't been invented or was outrageously expensive, I was working long hours manually printing labels, packing product, weighing packages, and standing in line at the post office every single day. It was a nightmare.

At that point I shut down my eBay business and started selling digital products that could be automatically delivered to the customer via download. After dealing with the hassles of eBay, information marketing seemed liked a fairytale. That same year I launched my first information product, a "how to" product about starting your own window-cleaning business. It wasn't a bad product for a first attempt, and I made a slight profit. But more importantly, I learned a lot from actually *doing it*. I learned firsthand about sales funnels, email lists, copywriting, conversion rates, and tracking your metrics.

I made lots of mistakes in the beginning and spent a ton of money, but it was all part of the learning process. It was also where I first learned about "modeling." I started looking at everyone else's websites, studying what was working and what they were doing to sell their products, and I decided to start modeling my business on what they were doing. I created similar products, wrote similar sales copy, made similar graphics, and then I held my breath and waited for the money to pour in.

It never did. Despite all of my stuff being VERY similar to what was working for other businesses, I was barely making enough to cover my expenses while they were raking in money hand over fist.

Honestly, it pissed me off, but luckily instead of throwing in the towel, I became a student of direct response online marketing. It took me several years to figure it all out, but finally, I realized there was more going on than met the eye in these other businesses.

In my ecom education company, we call it the Iceberg Effect. Two thirds of an iceberg's mass is hidden below the surface, unseen to the world. In online business, it's much the same: Two thirds of what makes a business successful occurs underneath the surface.

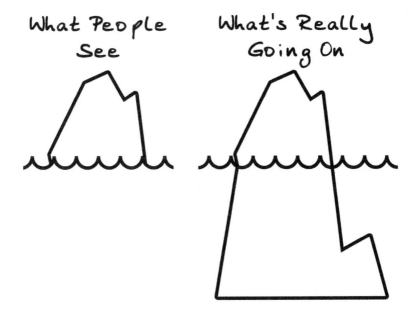

As I said, it took me years to figure this out. Once I did, my business went from barely breaking even to making millions of dollars per year in less than 12 months.

During this journey, being the serial entrepreneur that I am, I never stopped dabbling in ecommerce. As technology improved over the years, more and more of my time and energy went into selling physical products online.

This time, however, I took what I had learned in my information marketing business and applied those same direct response principles and strategies to my physical product brands, which was practically unheard of in the ecom industry. And as a result my ecom businesses exploded, my clients' businesses exploded, and suddenly everybody wanted to be my friend.

Fast forward to today. My ecom businesses are generating millions of dollars a year and are growing as rapidly as I will let them (you'll learn about sustainable growth rates later on in the book). Big-name companies pay me exorbitant sums to consult for their businesses. I also have the honor of consulting for and being an advisor to some of the fastest-growing ecom brands on the internet, and my ecom education and coaching company has helped thousands of students build their ecom stores in every market imaginable.

Why I Wrote This Book

Let me start by saying that I firmly believe that ecommerce is *the* business. Thanks to advances in technology, online globalization, and ease of access to manufacturers and suppliers, combined with the fact that as humans we love to buy *things* (and lots of them), ecommerce is one of the best businesses you could ever be in. Everything that was once a major barrier to entry into ecommerce has now evaporated.

Unfortunately, it's still an antiquated world that hasn't kept up with what is actually working in an online business. Most ecom business owners are still doing things in the same way they did in the early dotcom days. They focus their entire business on a storefront and think of ecommerce as nothing more than putting up an online catalog with a bunch of products and hoping those products sell.

It's that surface gloss from the Iceberg Effect. New entrepreneurs and business owners coming into the industry are all jumping in using training and information that's ten years behind, and I want to change that.

Ecommerce Evolved is my way of effecting that change.

Maybe you're just getting started in your ecom business. Maybe you own a business that's already running, but it's not doing well. Maybe your ecom brand is already the leader in its space. Regardless of where you are, I want you to read this book and think, *"Holy crap! I'm not even doing a tenth of this stuff!"* I want to show you how your business has limitless possibilities, or if you're new to the world of business, how simple it really is to build, grow, and scale a successful ecom business.

Why This Book Is Different

There's no shortage of marketing or business advice out there, some of it good, some of it bad. Some of it works for some businesses but not for others. In many cases, the only way to know for sure is to try it out for yourself.

And therein lies the problem (which *Ecommerce Evolved* solves). When they don't know exactly what to do, most people wind up all over the map trying, testing, and hoping something works. And that can burn through a ton of time and money before a solution emerges.

Let me give you a quick example. Suppose you approach a car and start pushing it. It doesn't move, and when you look to your right you see another, smaller car that looks like it weighs less and might move more easily. So you abandon the first car and start pushing on the second. Meanwhile, another person (your competition) comes by and starts pushing the car you left behind.

After several moments you realize the second car isn't going anywhere either, and you spot a third vehicle, an Audi R8 (those lightweight frames must surely make the Audi weigh less). So you leave the second car behind and start pushing the Audi.

Meanwhile, the other person is still pushing on the first car. At first it's not moving, just like when you tried to push it. But slowly and gradually, it begins to inch forward. It moves just a little bit at first. Then it moves a foot. The person keeps pushing, and the momentum starts to build. Now it's moving even faster and covering more distance.

You stop pushing the Audi to look at the first car. Now you're even more determined to get a car of your own moving forward, so you start on a fourth car that looks promising.

But the first car is picking up speed now. You're getting frustrated, so you look for lighter and lighter cars to push. But now you are tired and you eventually decide to call it quits.

When you turn to look at the first car, you notice both the first car and the person pushing it are nowhere in sight.

That analogy can be applied to your business as well.

When you spend all your time and money chasing strategy after strategy, you're not able to stay focused on your business or your goals.

When you have a proven plan—a system—in place, you're positioned to grow your business both over the short term AND the long term. That second person pushing the car had a proven plan, simple as it was, and they stuck with it.

Now if that person had had a tow truck, they surely could have moved it along much more quickly and with less effort on their part. But they had to start somewhere.

I want you to be that second person. My goal in writing *Ecommerce Evolved* is to give you both the proven plan AND the tow truck to build, grow, and scale a wildly profitable ecommerce business.

Four Distinctions That Set This Book Apart

1. The Vital Few

In the 1940s Dr. Joseph Juran recognized a universal principle he dubbed "The Vital Few and Trivial Many," which proved that roughly 20 percent of what is done is responsible for 80 percent of the results.[1] In recent years this has become known as the Pareto Principle and has proven true time and again in business. As the car analogy suggests, there are many different ways you can spend your time and money trying to grow your business, but it's important to focus on the right ones. *Ecommerce Evolved* simplifies that, since what you'll find in the following pages IS the "vital few"–the strategies, tactics, and methods that will deliver 80 percent of the results and catapult your success.

2. Zero Theory

You'll find zero theory inside *Ecommerce Evolved*. Most business authors write their book based on hypothetical

---

[1] (2009). Joseph Juran. *The Economist*. Retreived from http://www.economist.com/node/13881008

theories because they have no practical experience in what they are teaching.

The difference between me and most of my competitors is that I actually do this stuff every single day. I use every single strategy, tip, trick, and tactic I'm about to share with you on a daily basis to grow my ecommerce companies. I currently operate brands in three different major markets and I've used this stuff in dozens of other markets, from survival to supplements to kitchen accessories to heating and air conditioning products. Through Build Grow Scale (my ecommerce education company) and Black Label Mastermind (my elite ecommerce focus group for seven and eight-figure business owners), I also get to work with and advise hundreds of other businesses in practically every niche you can think of.

Everything you'll learn from *Ecommerce Evolved* is based on 100 percent real world, from-the-trenches results.

3. Evergreen Training

Chances are you've purchased a book or training that taught a method that became extinct when Google or Facebook or some other platform made a change. The content and training contained inside this book is evergreen and will not go out of date. What you learn in *Ecommerce Evolved* is timeless and will still be as relevant 10 years from now as it was the day I wrote it.

4. Systematic Immersion

This book is structured using a process called Systematic Immersion, which organizes information in such a way that it can be absorbed more effectively by the brain and also so that core topics or strategies are taught only after all the supporting elements have been covered. This ensures that you, the reader, will have not only an enjoyable experience consuming the information, but more importantly that you'll be ready and able to execute what you learned when you finish the book.

I recommend reading this entire book at least once from beginning to end before you take any action. You are diving below the surface to see the rest of the iceberg, and you need to understand the entire picture and how the pieces fit together. Once you've done that you can go back to whichever chapter, section, or topic you feel will give you the biggest win in your business.

With that said, let's dive in. I'm excited for you to see what lies underneath.

 You may access the members area with all resources here: http://ecommerceevolvedbook.com/customer-access

---

THE 12 CORE PRINCIPLES OF ECOMMERCE

After teaching upwards of 10,000 students and clients, I have discovered that most ecommerce owners have zero business training. Before these people started their ecom business, they may have been construction workers, nurses, or teachers. They get into business, not to *be* in business, but rather to make money. Then they find a product and think, "Cool! I'd love to sell this," and the rest is history.

I was once one of those people. I launched my first ecommerce business in 2001 with no prior experience, and I learned everything the hard way. Had I learned the contents of this book beforehand, I probably wouldn't be writing this book at all. I'd probably be living on my own tropical island somewhere instead.

Luckily, you don't need an MBA to run a successful ecommerce business, and you don't need to learn everything the hard way. The 12 Principles of Ecommerce you're about to read are all founded on timeless business principles, and I've updated them to make them more applicable to ecommerce businesses. These game-changing rules will help you understand the reasoning behind my teachings and lay the foundation for the rest of this book.

The concepts, strategies, and ideas in this book are different than the norm in ecommerce. Even if you have an MBA or already own a successful ecom business, you'll likely find that you are breaking one or more of these principles. If you're willing to be open-minded, this chapter could help you make some fundamental (and highly lucrative) improvements to your company.

1. Your Business is Not Unique

I want to get this principle out of the way first because it's one of the toughest pills for entrepreneurs to swallow. The reality is, **your business is not unique**. Your product may be unique, but the underlying business is not.

After hearing a particular strategy, the knee-jerk reaction for most people is, "My business is too unique to benefit from this." I hear that all the time from coaching students and clients; they all think their business is so special that my strategies don't apply to them.

I used to be the exact same way. My first ecommerce business sold heating HVAC supplies in the early days of eBay. I knew some very successful eBay sellers, but I never once asked them for help. I figured that since I sold HVAC supplies, someone selling floor mats or dog treats wouldn't be able to help me.

This is a common mistake for business owners and entrepreneurs. They almost always fail to ask for help because they believe their business is so unique that others can't understand it. Just remember that no matter how innovative your company is, there's somebody out there who can offer you some advice.

Contrary to what you might think, it's not about the product at all. All ecommerce businesses have systems for accounting, marketing, operations, sales, and the like. People don't say, "My business doesn't need accounting because my product is too unique," because they recognize that every business needs to have a solid accounting system. But people do say, "I can't buy my traffic on Facebook because my product is unique," or "I can't use a marketing system or a sales funnel because my product is too different."

In the end, those statements are just as ridiculous as the first one! If you realize that your business is not unique, you won't ignore solutions. If you insist on believing you're unique, you'll always struggle to achieve your goals. I don't want you to disregard my strategies and tactics just because you think you're a snowflake, so always remind yourself that *your business is not unique.*

2. Your Business is Marketing

If you don't make sales, it doesn't matter what you sell. You'll end up bankrupt. So regardless of what product you sell, *you're actually in the business of marketing.*

Like I mentioned in Principle 1, many ecommerce business owners focus on their product. They think, "I'm in the cutlery business, I'm not a marketer." The truth is, your business is marketing and the product is just the thing that you sell to generate revenue. Your niche or product is NOT your business.

I once worked with a couple that had a successful business in the custom jewelry space. They started on Etsy and they were moving over into an ecom store, and they had huge demand for their product. When I mapped out several different marketing campaigns and strategies for them, the husband was impressed, but the wife was adamant that they couldn't sell their product that way. She thought her customers didn't want to be marketed to, that all she and her husband had to do was show the world their art and wait for crowds to form.

Ultimately, this couple shot down every idea I suggested and I had to end my coaching relationship with them. They couldn't make the distinction between art and marketing.

Guess what happened? That couple's ecommerce business completely failed and they went back to selling on Etsy. Their business could have easily been doing $50,000 to $100,000 a month, and instead they are stuck making $5,000 to $10,000 a month on Etsy.

The lesson here is that you cannot hate marketing if you're in business! It's 100 percent a mentality issue. You may have the best product in a specific niche, but you can't be successful until you accept that your business is marketing and the product is just the thing you sell.

3. Brand Centric, Not Product Centric

As you just learned, you are in the business of marketing. A company that's focused on its product always struggles with customer acquisition and retention because the market needs something more: the message and the customer experience connected to a brand. So once you've accepted that you're in the business of marketing, focus on *building a message or movement that your customer can align with.*

When people start their business because of a specific product, all of their marketing decisions, all of their branding, everything they do becomes all about their product instead of their brand. This brings about mediocre results and a company that nobody cares about. Successful ecommerce businesses have branding and market messaging that fits their target market.

Your product is just a subset of your brand. There's no better way to get people to lower their guard online and purchase from you than by making them feel like they belong. Building a brand-centric focus helps you accomplish just that.

4. You Must Control the Order Process

Amazon, one of the biggest ecommerce platforms in the world, has a system called Fulfillment by Amazon (FBA) that allows entrepreneurs and business owners to sell their products on its platform. There's a lot of excitement around this system, and many people have built their "business" on Amazon.

People ignore the fact that Amazon owns the customer as well as the order process. When you send a customer to Amazon to buy your product, you become a glorified affiliate. It's your product, but Amazon just pays you a commission twice a month on sales.

Amazon is just one of many platforms that sell your product for you. When you use any of these channels, you don't control the order process. I don't discourage using those platforms, but if you use them exclusively, *you don't have a business*. Rather, you've built an income stream in someone else's back yard.

These platforms keep the customer data and control the entire sales cycle. You are legally not allowed to use the data AND you have no control over how the sales flow works. Any upsells or cross-sells are suggested by the platform, not you.

You can't effectively drive external traffic or marketing campaigns to an Amazon 'business' because you can't control or track the effectiveness of those campaigns. Why? *Because you don't control the order process.* You can't place any tracking or conversion pixels and discover that out of the twenty sales you made, five were from Facebook, three from YouTube, and the rest were organic. You don't have something scalable that you can control, that can weather the ups and downs of the marketplace. You can only cross your fingers and hope that you make more money than you spend on advertising and marketing.

Don't get me wrong, I've thrown lots of money at Amazon and I've made millions of dollars with the FBA program. I even had a couple of products on Amazon that made hundreds of thousands of dollars in sales every month, but when Amazon changed their search algorithm (which they do quite often), suddenly I was only making $30,000 in revenue a month.

I had already ordered and projected for hundreds of thousands of dollars' worth of inventory monthly, and now those products are just sitting in an Amazon warehouse accruing storage fees. Thankfully I also sell through other platforms where I have full control over the order process—otherwise my business would tank.

I've had accounts on Amazon shut down overnight. All I got was an email saying my account has been terminated, with no reason why this had happened and no contact information besides their email and phone support, which is as good as nothing.

I can think of dozens of other people to whom this has happened as well. I know people who were doing two million dollars a month in the health supplement space, only to have Amazon shut them down so it could sell the same product. It became a competitor and put them out of business.

Amazon does this fairly often. When the platform sees a product that's selling well, they can shut it down and ask for supplier data to verify that the product is legitimate. Once it has the information, Amazon contacts the supplier themselves, makes a huge order, and closes your account. It's a cutthroat world, and people who sell on Amazon need to consider that it could dry up at any moment.

Although I talk a lot about Amazon in this principle, it's not all about Amazon. The bottom line is this: **You need to control the order process**. In order to build a thriving ecommerce business, you must understand the function and flow of your sales cycles. You need to be able to test, tweak, and edit it at all times. You must be able to control everything—

product selection, payment processing, the receipt page, follow-up emails, everything. Afterwards you must own the customer data and be able to follow up with the customer.

If you don't control the order process, you can't do any of this. If you don't control the order process, you don't have a business.

Now I know it may sound like I hate Amazon and sites like it, but I don't. I love Amazon! Like I said, I have made millions of dollars selling my own products on the site. I also released one of the top online courses on how to create an income stream, sell, and launch products on Amazon. I am a big proponent of selling on the platform, but I am also not naïve enough to ever consider anything I do on Amazon a business. Amazon is just a sales channel for use *within* a business. I have my ecommerce store, and I also sell those same products on Amazon to scoop up more sales. It's an added bonus, not the foundation of my businesses.

5. Don't Compete on Price

Many business owners think that if they make their product cheaper, more people will buy it. But not only is competing on price bad for your bottom line, it makes prospects think that the only good thing about your product is the price, and that makes it really hard to build a brand and customer loyalty.

Competing on price is a race to the bottom. It means racing your competitor to lower prices until everyone is out of business and the product is basically free.

Somebody is always willing to lower their price below yours, so there's no such thing as a bottom threshold. In certain products and industries, Minimum Advertised Pricing

(MAP) prevents lowering prices past a certain price point, but even then, it's still a race to that lowest price point.

The entire electronics industry runs that way. TVs and other gadgets generally have the same price because there's no wiggle room. Merchants price everything as low as they can and make less than a 10 percent gross margin on the product.

The more you lower your price, the more your profit margin evaporates and when that happens, ecommerce store owners start cutting corners. First, they try to get the product for cheaper from their manufacturer or wholesaler. If the manufacturer is in China, they'll almost always agree to make it cheaper, but then the manufacturer also starts cutting corners. Soon you start putting out a substandard product. It's a vicious cycle that just gets worse and worse.

Competing on price turns your product into a commodity, and it's hard for an ecom business or startup to thrive on a commoditized product. Walmart thrives on commoditized products, but you can't compete with Walmart! You don't have the purchasing power, or the ability to leverage the economies of scale like they can.

When you sell a cheap product, you also end up attracting the worst kind of customers. They only buy one item, then they blow up your support team because the cheap product they bought didn't arrive the same day they bought it. They make your life a living hell.

Need another reason to avoid competing on price? When you're cheap, you blend into the background. People pick up on certain cues—confidence cues, social cues, pricing cues—before they even evaluate your product. If you compete on price, customers never get to that assessment of inherent value. They ignore you like they ignore people handing out free fliers on the street.

In the end, undercutting the competition is not worth doing. If your product can only compete on price, it's time to find new products. Either that or get used to living on Top Ramen.

6. Don't Be Walmart. Niche Down.

The wider your market is, the harder it'll be to grow your business. Be realistic: you have limited funds and you have to make the best return on investment (ROI) for your business that you can. Therefore, you need to *focus your efforts on a narrow and specific niche market that sells a specific subset of products.*

Let's go back to Walmart for a second. Walmart's model is to go wide. They're not in a niche at all. Walmart's market is *everyone*. They don't cater to fitness or health or beauty–they sell every product to every person.

Walmart can do that, but you can't. You're not an Amazon, you're not Walmart, and you're not even Cabela's. Unless you have tens of millions of dollars to spend on marketing and the capital for hundreds or thousands of SKU's worth of inventory, you won't have the means to compete. If you're venture funded and you're told to try it then by all means do so, but that's not a reality for most of us, and there are far better ways to spend your money.

There are several other issues to consider as well. Look at a mass niche retailer's marketing. They never actually market the benefits or the uniqueness of the product. They market on having the lowest prices, and you already know where that leads for smaller ecommerce businesses.

The other problem with a wide market is that you can't target ideal customers. How can you find them and show them your offer with your limited budget and marketing capacity?

Let's say you have a $1,000 marketing budget and your target is women. How many women will you reach, and how many will actually be interested in your product, much less buy it?

So, how do you go about targeting deep and not wide? Get specific! Consider the fitness market. As is, this market is way too broad; targeting "fitness" means you're targeting anyone from rock climbers to weight lifters. You could, however, niche down to something like mountain biking. You could even take it a step further and target something like downhill riding–people who like crashing down hills in the summer and at ski resorts. It's a specific, passionate subset of a market, and it's a good market–much better than fitness or general cycling.

However, you must be careful not to take this to the extreme. Niches like cat-patterned socks for men or underwater basket weaving are too small and obscure to be sustainable. While I'm sure there's someone out there in the world who likes to basket weave while sitting on the bottom of the ocean, it's not a sizeable enough market for you to build a business.

But generally, this is not too much of a concern. I've never had a client who scaled down too much. Most try to go broad, and the ones that do niche down oftentimes don't niche down as far as they should.

Let's walk through how this works. You have a $1,000 budget and most of your products are for mountain bikers, but your niche is cycling. If you spend your $1,000 targeting people who like cycling and bicycling, a good chunk of your target market may be kids or road bike fanatics who can't stand mountain bikes. Only a fraction of the people you reach will actually be interested in mountain bikes.

If, instead, you build your niche and your site around specifically downhill mountain bikers, you can focus that same

$1,000 specifically on downhill mountain bikers. You've narrowed your focus and niched down instead of widening, and now your marketing dollars go farther with a much higher ROI.

This happened to a client of mine who wanted to get into the yoga market. His products were exclusively associated with Bikram Yoga (hot yoga), but all the branding and messaging on his site was all about regular yoga. There's a huge difference between Bikram Yoga and regular yoga (one is very sweaty and the other one is just Zen), and the Bikram Yoga market is much more passionate than the broader yoga market.

When I started working with this client, I helped him change his branding, company image, advertising, message, everything to exclusively target Bikram Yoga. Sales increased upwards of 57 percent almost immediately.

This guy went from wide to deep, and he reaped the benefits. So can you.

7. No Such Thing as Free Traffic

I think each generation of entrepreneurs gets more and more entitled. They want to set up a business, but they don't want to put any money in advertising. They want lots of free traffic to magically show up and then, poof! They're in business and money is pouring from the sky.

I know this because I used to be one of those entitled entrepreneurs. Back in 2001 and 2002, I created a business that sold window cleaning products. I also created some products to teach window cleaners how to start a business (you may recall from the introduction that I used to be a window cleaner).

I lived on savings at the time, so the whole free traffic SEO thing sounded perfect. I spent hours and hours learning about keyword research and similar tactics to help my site get more attention on Google. But I never actually took into consideration the actual volume of traffic that was available. At the time, the global search volume on Google for my primary keyword was only 25 visitors a month (I'm not joking). As you can imagine, this did not make me rich.

Today the traffic pool is much larger, but the concept still holds. The problem is that marketers and business trainers know that the word "free" works like magic, so they play on that. "Free traffic" as a sales message works so well because most people are risk averse, but they still need money.

That's why people focus on Search Engine Optimization (SEO) and Public Relations (PR). They spend hundreds of hours a month trying to get Google to send them customers. They may not be spending money, but they are still spending *time*, which is actually more valuable than money.

SEO or content marketing, as with all things, has a cost. While it may not be a financial cost, the time cost is HUGE. Not only are you not making sales if you're waiting for traffic to show up; you also won't get any meaningful data from a trickle of website visitors. If you don't get a sizable amount of data, you can't make good decisions or changes that'll generate revenue for your company.

The free traffic mentality also causes business owners to turn a blind eye to paid traffic. Many people think it's a bad idea to pay for traffic, but that's just flat-out wrong. When you buy traffic, you get it *immediately* and you can run tests, get relevant statistical data, and make more money. I'm not saying SEO is bad, but it's certainly not the end-all-be-all that many business owners think it is.

8. Business Costs Money

If you're already in business, you probably already know this, but here's a reminder: It costs money to make money. That's part of business. If you're not willing to spend money in your business, go get a job.

Ecommerce businesses have less overhead than most brick-and-mortar businesses, but that doesn't make them free to operate. There are still fees for hosting, processing, inventory, advertising, legal services...the list goes on and on. Come to terms with this and don't go cheap on your business.

There are a lot of cheapskates who are so afraid of spending money that they don't invest enough in their businesses, only to have those ventures flounder. It's okay to be budget conscious, but being cheap about building, growing, or scaling your business dooms you to failure.

The most common spending problem ecommerce business owners have is with advertising. Before the dotcom boom, some markets spent hundreds or thousands of dollars per month on yellow page phone book ads. Many entrepreneurs don't think twice about buying one of my $997 courses or my $5,000 workshop, but then they refuse to spend more than $10 per day on an advertising campaign!

You have to be willing to spend money, knowing some of it (such as investments in marketing tests) will not be recovered. If you have to choose, forego the personal luxuries and use the money for your business. This reaps the biggest rewards. As author Dave Ramsey says, "Live like no one else now so later you can *live* like no one else."[2]

---

[2] (2012, July 24). Tired of Keeping Up with the Joneses? Retrieved from https://www.daveramsey.com/blog/tired-of-keeping-up-with-the-joneses/

9. If You're Not Mobile, You're Out

Ecommerce is surprisingly archaic. Many ecom entrepreneurs still have that brick-and-mortar mentality towards their business, and up until the end of 2013, ecom companies could get away with ignoring mobile.

Not anymore. At this point, ignoring mobile is like signing your store's death warrant. In the beginning of 2014, the number of mobile internet users surpassed the number of fixed-access internet users.[3] Mobile internet usage is now *larger* than non-mobile internet usage. In 2015 alone, mobile users accounted for 29.7 percent of all U.S. ecommerce sales.[4] Nearly 30 percent of the U.S. ecommerce sales were made using mobile devices in 2015, and that number is expected to TRIPLE by the end of 2016.[5]

Here's the deal: *you need to make mobile traffic a primary consideration in your business.* At a minimum, your ecommerce store needs to have a responsive design (a design that is readable and functional on mobile). This should only be the starting point, since responsive design is like slapping a new coat of paint on a house you're trying to sell. It helps, but it's not enough to actually sell the house.

Let me give you some numbers from one of by businesses to make this more real for you. 44 percent of one of my largest site's traffic comes from mobile. 38 percent of our front-end sales and 23.33 percent of our repeat purchases come from mobile. If we didn't cater to mobile visitors, we'd be losing almost 40 percent of our sales, and that's just one of my stores.

---

[3] https://www.comscore.com/Insights/Blog/Major-Mobile-Milestones-in-May-Apps-Now-Drive-Half-of-All-Time-Spent-on-Digital

[4] https://www.internetretailer.com/2015/08/18/mobilecommerce-now-30-all-us-ecommerce

[5] http://www.emarketer.com/Article/Mobile-Payments-Will-Triple-US-2016/1013147

You can't ignore that many potential buyers and expect to remain successful for long. Mobile interactions **must** be a major priority of your business, and you need to get on board or drown.

10. The One Who Can Spend the Most to Acquire a Customer Wins

Ecommerce businesses have some of the highest customer acquisition costs of any business. Acquiring a brick-and-mortar retail customer costs about half as much as acquiring a customer online.[6] So, naturally, most ecom business owners want to get customers for the lowest possible price. They spend $6 to acquire a customer, then spend all their time figuring out how to get that down to $3. Even some of my high-level Mastermind members, who run multimillion-dollar companies, have this issue.

Here's the thing: *if you can't afford to buy your customers, you don't have a business.* Your competition has the same constraints as you do. It's expensive for them to acquire customers too, and they have the same crappy shopping cart conversion rates that you do. Your competition is probably also trying to get customers as cheaply as possible.

Don't be like the competition! A higher cost of customer acquisition is not a problem for businesses that are optimized to withstand it. If you focus on how to engineer your business so that you can spend more to acquire a customer and still be profitable, you can blow your competition away. You can grow your business exponentially and enjoy a healthy 40 to 80 percent annual growth rate year after year with no adverse effects.

---

[6] State of Retailing 2009, Forrester Research (shop.org)

One rule of thumb when it comes to spending is to *be willing to spend up to your customer lifetime value (LTV) to acquire a customer.* This works for some companies, but in my experience it's a little aggressive. Also, since most companies don't even know what their customer LTV is, it's somewhat impossible to do accurately.

I prefer to use a figure that is easier to calculate: *the 60-day valuation of a customer.* How much does your average customer spend in 60 days, including repeat purchases and subscriptions? Calculate that number and know that you can spend up to that amount to acquire a customer (anything beyond that average value is profit).

Creating the Highest Average Customer Value

The higher your average customer value is, the more you can spend to acquire a customer. Maybe your average customer value was $5, but if you tweaked your funnels and increased it to $25. Now you can spend $20 more than you could before to acquire a customer. That doesn't mean you'll spend that max amount, but you *can* spend up to $25 to acquire a customer.

Optimizing your business to create the highest average customer value allows you to tap into traffic sources that were initially too expensive for you. Maybe, when your customer value at 60 days was $5, you found a source to buy traffic for $5 a customer and got 10 sales a day. You saw another traffic source that was more expensive and you could get significantly more traffic, but you couldn't afford it due to your low ACV.

When your average customer value goes up, everything changes. You can buy traffic and advertising that costs up to your new limit. Your competition won't be able to do that because they, like most business owners, are probably still focused on trying to get customers as inexpensively as possible.

Be Careful Not to Overspend

Principle 10 is, "The One Who CAN Spend the Most to Acquire a Customer Wins," not "The One Who DOES Spend the Most to Acquire a Customer Wins." Yes, you should structure your business so that you can afford to spend increasing amounts to acquire a customer. That does not mean you should spend everything you can to acquire customers.

Consistently breaking even to acquire a customer sounds great in theory, but as an ecom business scales past the first few million dollars a year in sales, you face a new problem: cash flow. Ecom businesses notoriously have lousy cash flow because large amounts of money get stuck in the supply chain cycle. Factor in customer acquisition that takes 30, 60, or 90 days to ROI and you'll find yourself in a serious cash flow pinch that could prevent you from scaling and even wipe you out.

As your business gets into the high seven to eight-figure range, other business expenses arise and grow rapidly as well. Continuing to spend the maximum amount on customer acquisition may harm you, it is for this reason that budgeting is critical to the growth of your business. For more information on how to balance the two, see my video on the subject (located in the resources section in the member's area).

11. Sell in Multiple Channels

We live in a global economy without boundaries. Search technology is progressing by leaps and bounds, so when people type in your product, they'll typically find it. And the more places they find your product, the more money you'll make.

By channels, I mean places that your product is actually sold. The most common sales channels are your ecommerce store, Amazon, eBay, and offline retail stores. None of these channels are new businesses; they are simply add-on cash flows, not a substitute for your main ecommerce store (see Principle 4).

Multiple sales channels generate more money. They help you make more sales and improve your economies of scale (the more product you sell, the more products you order from your manufacturer; the larger your order, the lower your volume pricing per unit).

This is all partially because multi-channel selling changes customer perception. It makes you look bigger and more trustworthy. It disguises you, even if you are just a small merchant working out of the spare bedroom of your mom's house.

I recommend the two-channel approach in most cases: Your ecommerce store and Amazon FBA. This is because, firstly, Amazon is an amazing cash flow addition to your business. Done right, it can make up 30–40 percent of your income, or even more in certain markets. It's a great way to increase profit without having to increase your product line.

Secondly, many customers visit niche retailer sites but don't buy. Many times, they've never heard of you before and are not comfortable with your store, but they like the product. If they find your product on Amazon (even if you retarget or send them to Amazon yourself), they may buy your product because they trust Amazon. The next time they buy, there's a much higher chance they'll buy directly from you because they now trust you.

One word of caution: As you learned in Principle 4, you don't have a business unless you control the order process. None of the channels I mentioned here allow you to control the order process. Use them for better positioning and more money, and that's it. Don't treat them like businesses. Instead, focus your efforts on the actual business that you control and use the multiple channels to soak up extra cash.

12. There Are Only Three Ways to Grow a Business

Marketing legend Jay Abraham spearheaded the idea that there are only three ways to grow your business. Not four, six, or eighteen, just three. I've found it to be true in every business I've ever run. Those three ways are:

1) **Get more customers.** Most ecommerce businesses do a good job focusing on this. It's the only thing they seem to care about.

2) **Increase the size of your orders.** Get your customers to spend more money when they purchase. Some stores do this well, but it's often overlooked or only halfheartedly attempted.

3) **Increase the order frequency.** Get your customers to buy more often, turning a one-time buyer into a two-time buyer and so on. The more repeat purchases you have, the more money you make.

Most ecommerce businesses rely solely on #1 (customer acquisition). They either ignore or expend too few resources pursuing the other two, much to their detriment. The business owners who make that mistake don't realize that it's five times more expensive to acquire a new customer than it is to sell to an old customer.[7]

Acquiring 1 new customer costs the same as retaining 5 existing customers

Back when I was first diving into this type of stuff, I learned in a training seminar that focusing on any one of these three areas grows your business in a linear fashion, but even small growth in each of the three areas together results in geometric growth. For example, if you get a 10 percent increase in each of these three categories, it results in a 33 percent (not 30 percent) growth bump to your business and your bottom line.[8] The image below shows how this works.

Increase the # of Clients		Increase the Average $ per Sale		Increase the Repurchase Frequency		Total
1000	*	100	*	2	=	$200,000
10% Increase		10% Increase		10% Increase		33% Increase
1100	*	110	*	2.2	=	$266,200

A 10% increase in each of the three areas equals a 33% increase in revenue

---

[7] Lee Resources Inc. via Forbes
(http://www.forbes.com/sites/alexlawrence/2012/11/01/five-customer-retention-tips-for-entrepreneurs/#2fb5c53417b0)

[8] http://www.slideshare.net/loanfinder/jay-abrahams-power-parthanon

Once you understand this, you'll never look at business the same way. The rest of this book is dedicated to helping you maximize all three of these growth areas in your business.

Conclusion

Thanks for bearing with me. I wanted to get these principles out of the way first because they set the stage for everything else you'll learn, for all the tactical and strategic information in the next three sections of the book.

Now that you've learned these principles, you'll understand my thought process as you read on. You'll recognize these principles again and again in each chapter, shaping the way successful ecommerce businesses work. If you take them to heart, everything else falls into place.

The 12 Core Principles of Ecommerce

1. Your Business Is Not Unique

2. You Are in the Business of Marketing

3. Brand Centric, Not Product Centric

4. You Must Control the Order Process

5. Don't Compete on Price

6. Don't Be Walmart. Niche down.

7. There's No Such Thing as Free Traffic

8. Business Costs Money

9. If You Aren't Mobile, You're Out

10. The One Who Can Spend the Most to Acquire a Customer Wins

11. Sell in Multiple Channels

12. There Are Only Three Ways to Grow a Business

PART I

● ●

EVOLVED
STRATEGY

Things have changed since the early dotcom days. The internet has exploded, technology has progressed, and consumers have gotten savvier. All of these things have evolved, and that means you, the ecom business owner, need to evolve too.

The problem is that most ecom businesses have not evolved. They are still structured and operated in the same archaic way that they were when ecommerce took off in the early 2000s. A lot of the ecom people came from the brick-and-mortar retail world–they simply got online and started copying successful online stores. It's very much a monkey-see-monkey-do approach.

The problem is–and this is inherent to 90 percent of the population–we take in only a surface-level view of what's actually going on. As I mentioned in the introduction, it's like an iceberg. You don't see what's going on under the surface that's actually driving that business.

The business owners who try to copy successful ecommerce businesses don't see all of the integral parts that actually make those businesses successful. Additionally, business is *hard*. It's complicated and there are a zillion moving pieces that you have to deal with all the time. Most business owners are so caught up in that daily grind that they can only do what they're already doing, whether it's working or not with no time to look at anything new.

In Part 1, my goal is to pull back the curtain, take you behind the scenes, and show you how ecommerce businesses really work. In this section, You'll learn the strategies, structures, tactics, and all the different pieces that help build, grow, and scale an ecommerce business. Best of all, the strategies in this section are applicable to everyone. Whether you're starting a business or you're already making millions of dollars a month, you'll learn something essential in the following pages.

CHAPTER 1

FUNNEL-BASED ECOMMERCE

This chapter will shake up your understanding of the ecommerce world and really test your belief that you can actually use my ideas in your business. The information you'll find here is very contrary to common ecommerce thought and the average person's perception of a business. As you read this chapter, remember Principle 1 (your business is not unique) and Principle 2 (you are in the marketing business); they will help you accept the truths that many ecommerce entrepreneurs fail to grasp.

In this chapter, you'll learn why you should focus your ecommerce business, not around your ecommerce store, but around sales funnels. We will cover what makes sales funnels so effective, the different components, types of sales funnels, and how to implement sales funnels in your business starting today. Sales funnels are a big part of my success, and if you give them a chance, they could soon be a big part of yours.

Here's one final, important point before we dive in: *You should never spend any customer acquisition marketing efforts or dollars on sending visitors to your online store.*

I'm not just saying this for effect. I currently own three ecommerce brands and all three have experienced exponential growth since adopting this policy. If you keep an open mind, by the end of this chapter you'll be ready to adopt the same policy except in two specific cases, which we'll discuss in the evolved marketing section. No, I'm not crazy, and yes, I did just tell you not to send traffic to your ecom stores.

The Two Worlds of Ecommerce

In the early days of ecommerce, most business owners exclusively stuck to shopping carts (essentially an online version of a mail order catalog). When shopping, customers would find their product, click on it to view the product detail page, and then click on the checkout button. The store might suggest other items and other minor additions, but this was the basic template of every single ecommerce store.

Back then, there were two types of ecommerce businesses: online stores that sold physical products, and direct-response information marketers who sold information via courses, ebooks, and training products. The latter type of ecommerce evolved from the offline direct response world, where marketers mailed sales letters advertising courses. When these marketers got online, they brought what was working offline with them—and just like that, the online sales funnel was born.

At first, online stores and online sales funnels were completely separate. The ecom retailers thought the marketers were spammers, and the marketers thought the retailers didn't understand business. But over time, both parties loosened up.

The current ecommerce world is a combination of these two approaches. Direct response marketing businesses are now incorporating the use of shopping carts in select instances, and successful ecommerce businesses are leveraging direct response-style sales funnels. As you might expect, both parties are doing better as a result.

Why Funnel-Based Ecommerce is So Effective

Ecommerce used to suck. When it first started and the technology was in its infancy, it was a manual process that took massive amounts of time to set up.

You might remember from the introduction that I started reselling HVAC products on eBay 2001, and in 2002 I started learning about sales funnels. I then abandoned ecommerce and went into information marketing. After building many sales funnels for my information marketing business from 2003 to 2011, advances in ecommerce technology piqued my interest again. I got into Amazon and started selling products.

When I built my new ecommerce stores, it was a no-brainer to use sales funnels due to their ability to boost sales and profits. I never let the fact that I was selling a physical product stop me from using a funnel; I knew I could control so much more of the customer experience and greatly boost my business with them. I used a storefront as well, and merging the two worlds came naturally, leading to a hybrid model.

This hybrid immediately led to more profitability and rapid growth. I beat my competition and scaled each of my companies to multi-million dollar brands in *less than one year*. The use of sales funnels completely transformed my business.

The Proof Is in the Numbers

You are likely already very aware that shopping cart conversion rates on average are pathetic. On average, ecommerce shopping carts convert around 1 percent on the front end.[9] If 100 people visit an ecom store, only one person buys something.

Yes, you can get higher conversion rates, especially on platforms like Amazon, and with some tweaking you can increase your storefront's average conversion rate. But on a traditional storefront, 1 percent conversion is the global average.

That's what makes sales funnels so fantastic by comparison. In my experience, even a basic sales funnel has conversion rates that are 3 to 5 percent higher than traditional storefront conversion rates. By building a sales funnel and sending traffic to it (assuming you have a marketing budget), you increase the ROI for every advertising dollar you spend right from the start. This self-funds further customer acquisition, helping your business grow.

Sales funnels also **massively** increase average order value. Most ecom stores typically rely on automated scripts that display suggested or related items to increase order value, but

---

[9] http://index.fireclick.com/fireindex.php

that's far from ideal–for most of my clients, the average conversion rate from suggested items at checkout is less than 5 percent. It's better than nothing, but it won't dramatically increase the growth of your company. Sales funnels, on the other hand, make going to your ecommerce store like going to Target: people walk in to buy milk and come out with a shopping cart full of things they didn't even know they needed.

I know that was a lot of information, so if you remember anything from this section, remember this. A basic ecommerce sales funnel *boosts average order value by 20 percent*. An advanced multi-step ecommerce funnel can *boost average order value by over 60 percent*–and that's just on the initial purchase. Add repeat purchases and lifetime value to the equation, and your revenues go through the roof.

The Buyer's High

Why are sales funnels so much more effective than a traditional online storefront? It's because sales funnels capitalize on the buyer's high, a dopamine rush customers get when they purchase something.

When that dopamine rush hits, the consumer brain is primed with 'feel good' chemicals and is the most receptive it will ever be to additional purchases. That's your **best chance** to get people to buy additional items, and because the sales funnel offers these additional items right in this window of optimal timing, they work very well.

The buyer's high also makes selling recurring billing products and subscriptions much easier. Selling continuity-type offers on the front end is difficult, especially with new customers (since they don't trust you yet). But if you position the recurring billing as an upsell after customers make their purchase, the trust factor is higher since they've already made the initial purchase and therefore the chance of getting them to buy something else dramatically increases. That's why with sales funnels, you can rapidly scale your ecommerce business at a rate that you never thought possible.

I have a group called Black Label Mastermind for my highest-level ecom clients, the ones who already make millions of dollars per year. One of the members is an apparel seller who primarily deals with t-shirts. When he joined Black Label, he had an average cart value of $31. When we added a simple sales funnel to his business, his average cart size immediately increased by 16 percent.

After tweaking the funnel, we got a 22.58 percent cart value increase within 30 days. His average cart value went up from $31 to $38–that's an additional $7 per order. With his first 1,000 sales using the optimized sales funnel, he brought in an impressive $7,000 in additional cart revenue.

If that doesn't sound great enough as it is, let's look at this from the perspective of Principle 10 (The One Who Can Spend the Most to Acquire a Customer Wins). That's an additional $7 this business owner can now spend on average to acquire each customer. That money can be used to acquire EVEN MORE customers for more profits, leading to massive growth.

Pieces of a Sales Funnel

Hopefully you're now sold on the idea of a sales funnel and want to know how to build your own. But before you try to build one, you first need to know how sales funnels are put together and structured.

Most sales funnels have the same basic components. Not all of these components are necessary for each funnel, and there are some more exotic components that won't be mentioned here, but by and large, the following pieces are the ones you need to know about.

Front End

This is the landing page where you send traffic. These pages are most often configured as a sales letter or review page.

I call these pages Buy, Bookmark, or Leave (BBL) pages, as they are a dedicated offer page designed to sell just ONE of your core products without any of the other distractions of your ecommerce store. There are no categories, additional products, navigation links, or visual elements that could lure your prospective buyer away from completing their purchase.

On a front-end landing page, people only have three choices: buy the item, bookmark the page, or leave. This is why dedicated front-end landing pages that bypass your standard product page can boost your sales conversions by 5 to 10 percent.

Order Bump

An order bump is a special offer designed to increase the average order value BEFORE the customer checks out and is shown any upsells or one-time offers. The product offered during this stage is similar to whatever product the customer is buying. It can be a bundle of digital products (such as videos and guides), a lifetime warranty, or a physical product that complements the main purchase.

An order bump appears on the checkout page, right above the payment section or below the cart details section. There's no big "add to cart" button or multiple pages they have to click through; it's clean and simple. It's just a little blurb of text, maybe an image of the product, and a checkbox to indicate they want the 'bump' that increases (or "bumps") a customer's cart value before they check out.

A great strategy commonly used by businesses in the nutraceutical niche (a portmanteau of the words "nutrition" and "pharmaceutical") is to *automatically* add an order bump to the cart. When a customer looks at the items in their cart, the order bump appears as the last item on the list. It's highlighted to make it obvious that it's an automatic addition.

If you do this, always tell the customer that if they don't want the additional product, they can simply uncheck the box. If a customer doesn't want it, they uncheck the box and the addition vanishes. Many people get surprised when this happens and suddenly feel like they're missing out, so they instinctively recheck the box and complete their purchase with the bump.

I use order bumps all the time. In my t-shirt business, I offer customers who buy my t-shirts an order bump of three custom stickers for $9.99. The stickers have the same design as the t-shirt, and these designs are always niche specific. If someone wants a t-shirt with the design, they'll probably want the stickers too. This particular order bump has a 21 percent take rate on average, meaning that out of 100 orders, 21 people add the order bump to their order and provide us with an additional $209.79 in revenue.

Upsell

The upsell comes after the customer has checked out, while the payment is processing but before the customer is redirected to the confirmation page. The perfect example of an upsell we're all familiar with is, "Would you like fries with that?"

FRONTEND   UPSELL

You want your customers to buy something else, and that something should be closely related to whatever the customer is already buying. If they buy a yoga mat, for example, the upsell could be a yoga towel or a yoga mat carrier. You can have more than one upsell in a sequence; you could try to sell them the yoga towel *and* the yoga mat carrier. You can also try to sweeten the deal by offering a discount on the upsell product.

A successful ecommerce funnel uses "one-click" payment technology in the upsell so the customer doesn't have to enter their payment details again. There should be a button that says "Click to add to order" that, when clicked, automatically charges the customer's card and adds the item to their order. This is **vital** because forcing customers to re-enter their payment details during the upsell sequence reduces the upsell conversion rate by as much as 30 percent.

Upsells milk that dopamine rush from the buyer's high; anything that slows down the process results in a lower conversion rate. As the customer enters their details again, they get time to think about whether they need that extra related product, which is bad for your conversion rates.

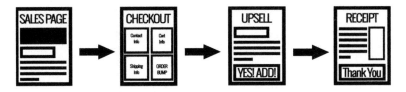

Downsell

The downsell is a simpler or cheaper offer than the upsell. It's only shown to the customer if they say no to the upsell because it's generally a better offer than the upsell, an attempt to snag the customer even if they refuse the upsell.

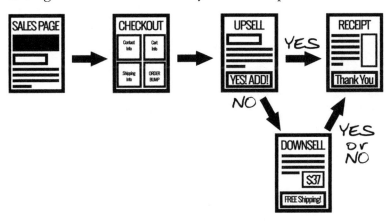

There are several distinct kinds of downsells:

- Reducing the price of the upsell. If you offer a yoga mat carrier for $25 on your upsell and the customer refuses, you can offer it for $20 instead. If you offered a 20 percent discount on the yoga mat carrier as an upsell and the customer refused, offer a better discount as a downsell. You're essentially haggling to get the customer to buy more.

- Offer a different product entirely. Instead of the yoga mat carrier, offer yoga mat cleaning solution.

- Offer free shipping.

You could have a downsell for every upsell if you wanted to, but that could get annoying for the customer. I try not to have more than two to three upsells and one downsell offer in a funnel sequence. You want to guide your customer through your sales process, but you also want them to come back and buy from you later. If the upsell sequence is too complicated, not only do they not come back, but they may go out of their way to trash you on social media.

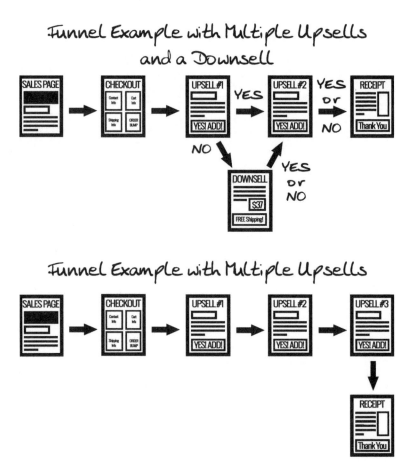

Recurring Income Offer (RIC Offer)

If you have a subscription or a recurring revenue program—we'll discuss these at length in the next chapter—create an upsell or one-time offer where you give your customers a chance to join your program with one click. This is another default standard offer you can include in a funnel. If you have a recurring income program in your business, then it should be a mandatory part of every funnel you offer.

Products

Products aren't part of the anatomy of a sales funnel, but you've probably noticed that each component of the funnel (front end, order bump, upsell, and downsell) needs a product to function. Assuming you already have at least two products, I want you to *position what you already have in a sales funnel,* one product in front of the other, in order to increase sales. You don't have to offer new products; just try to sell more of what you already have.

As you just learned, one product goes on the front end and additional products appear as upsells as customers go through the sales funnel. You need a core product to push on the front and one to three complementary products that are similar to your core product to offer as potential upsells. Make your best-selling product from your store your front-end product because if it's selling well, you can make it sell even better with a dedicated sales page on the front of a funnel.

Let me give you an example. Say your best-selling product is a flashlight. When you make it your front-end product, the complementary upsell products could be rechargeable batteries or a battery charger.

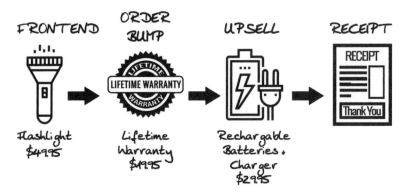

This is another reason why niching down is so important (refer to Principle 6: Don't Be Walmart). If you have a wide product line, it's hard to find related products. The more focused your product line is, the better funnels will work for you.

Traditional marketing wisdom dictates that funnels go from least expensive to most expensive, but that's not always the case for ecommerce sales funnels. You may decide to go from a $60 front-end product to a $14 order bump and then a $36 upsell. If that's what makes the most sense for your funnel and related items, do it. I mix up my price points all the time to make them work in my funnels and you should do the same.

The Two Types of Ecom Funnels

Now that you understand how funnels are structured, let's discuss the different types of funnels. There are two main types of ecommerce funnels: the stand-alone funnel and the upsell funnel path. It's not one or the other; you ideally should be using both.

The Stand-Alone Funnel

The stand-alone funnel is a way to get people to really focus. It's a collection of web pages that usher the customer through a structured sales process *without directing them to your storefront.* It bypasses your store completely.

When a customer clicks on your ad or email and is directed to a stand-alone funnel, they go through without ever visiting a storefront or product listing page and clicking "add to cart." The stand-alone funnel always includes these components:

1) **A landing page that sells the front-end product**. It can be a written sales page, a video, or a combination of both.

2) **A checkout page where the customer enters their payment details**. Ideally this should be a single-page checkout. Even if you have a multiple-step checkout on your store, use a single-page checkout for your sales funnel. Most stores support custom checkout pages for specific items.

3) **The upsells and downsells.** Each upsell has its own sales page featuring whatever additional related product you want your customer to buy. Like the landing page, these pages can have text or video elements. Every stand-alone sales funnel needs to have at least one upsell, but ideally it should have at least two. I use three in my business. You can use more if you like, but this may negatively affect the customer's experience.

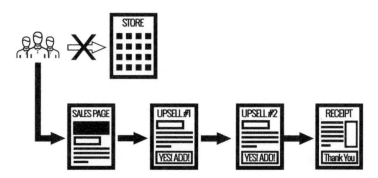

You should **always direct all of your external marketing efforts into a stand-alone sales funnel**. These are specifically designed to maximize front-end conversions and increase your cart size.

I mentioned earlier that you shouldn't deliberately send any traffic to your store, and that's because you should send it to your stand-alone sales funnel instead. You'll get a higher conversion rate, larger cart size, more money, and far more customers this way.

Once a customer purchases through the stand-alone sales funnel, you can send them to your storefront via email for repeat purchases. Stand-alone funnels require some work to set up (it can take a couple of days or weeks), but as you can see, the rewards are HUGE once they are in place.

The Upsell Funnel Path

The upsell funnel path, unlike the stand-alone funnel, is attached to your ecommerce store. It's automatically activated when a customer makes a purchase.

When someone goes to your website, browses through your products, adds one to their cart, and checks out, the upsell funnel path begins. It ends before the customer sees a receipt page. There's no front-end on an upsell funnel path—it starts with the first upsell and ends with the last upsell or downsell.

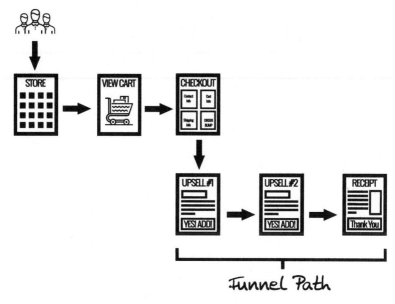

Funnel Path

Almost all ecommerce platforms now have upsell path functionality either built in or as an add-on application. Even if you have to add an application, upsell paths are *much* easier to set up than stand-alone sales funnels. You should be able to implement them on the same day you read this chapter.

At the same time, upsell funnels aren't quite as effective as stand-alone funnels. Not as many customers will see the upsell funnel path because an ecommerce store's front-end conversions are so much lower than those of a stand-alone funnel. Even so, upsell funnel paths are worth using because they're very easy to set up and they work wonders for your store's average cart value.

There are three types of upsell funnel paths: default, product-specific, and behavioral-based. Different storefronts support different types of upsell funnel paths (Magento,

Shopify, UltraCart, or Big Commerce, for instance). Most stores support having multiple upsell paths in your store, and if yours does, you can use specific upsell funnel paths that are triggered when particular products are purchased.

Default Upsell Funnel Paths

I suggest you use a blanket default upsell funnel path that positions best-selling products as upsells. This is the first upsell funnel path you should create. It should be automatically applied to *every single purchase* made in your store, regardless of what product is purchased or whether or not you use other upsell funnel paths. Once you set up the default upsell funnel path, your store will automatically show it as long as there is no other upsell path specified. This way no matter what product is purchased, the customer will always see some type of upsell sequence that encourages them to increase the size of their order.

Product-Specific Upsell Funnel Paths

A product-specific upsell funnel path is a designated upsell sequence that is triggered when a specific product is purchased from the store. They convert higher than a default funnel because they're more tightly related to the front-end purchase. Say you run an outdoors store that sells flashlights, pocket knives, tents, and the like. If a customer buys a flashlight, a product-specific upsell funnel path offers them appropriate accessories, such as batteries. If they bought a pocket knife, you might set up a specific funnel path that offers them a special deal on a knife sharpener. If they bought a tent and you don't have specific accessories that go with it, the default upsell funnel activates.

Behavior-Based Upsell Funnel Paths

Behavior-based funnels are only offered in more advanced shopping cart platforms. They can be quite complex and difficult to set up, but that's because they are SO much more sophisticated.

Behavior-based funnels actually *customize their responses to the purchasing behavior of the customer.* It uses what is called "if-then tagging," which allows you to set up specific rules in advance that tell your store what upsells to show or not show. This customizes the funnel on the fly based on what you know about the customer.

So let's say this time the customer bought the flashlight and the pocket knife. The behavior-based funnel would know to use the rechargeable batteries and charger as one upsell and the knife sharpener as another upsell. The behavior-based funnel also remembers customer history (everything someone has ever purchased) and uses these rules to avoid offering people upsells of products they've already purchased, even years in the future. This is helpful if you have lots of repeat customers.

Behavior-based upsell funnel paths can have better results than the other types of upsell funnel paths, but only when set up correctly, and setting them up correctly can be a complicated and time-consuming process. But the more volume you have, the more important it is to have a behavioral-based upsell funnels in place. It absolutely pays for itself in the long run.

I use a behavioral-based upsell funnel path in my hunting and outdoors business. That brand is now in its fifth year, and for the first four years, we used default and product-specific funnel paths while focusing heavily on increasing our repeat business.

By the time we hit our fifth year, I had many repeat customers who had already bought most of the products in my upsell sequences. I didn't want to show repeat customers products they already owned, so we upgraded to use only behavioral-based upsells for that business.

I encountered so many issues trying to set up the behavioral sequences that I ended up hiring an outside tech team, but it was worth it! After we started using behavioral-based upsells, our average cart value on our repeat purchases climbed almost 30 percent. And with the volume of sales we do on a daily basis, I can tell you that it makes a BIG difference for our bottom line.

Incorporating Sales Funnels into Your Business

Now that we've covered the different types and components of sales funnels, as well as what makes them so valuable, let's discuss incorporating these super-effective sales funnels into your business. First, as I already mentioned, *create a stand-alone funnel for your best-selling product.* Add the accessories that go with it as upsells or downsells in the funnel.

Once you've done that, get traffic to that product, check your conversions, and optimize each step of the funnel. Only when your funnel is converting profitably and consistently should you move on to your second-best selling product and duplicate the process.

Do this over and over until all your best-selling products have dedicated stand-alone funnels. Every time you roll out a new funnel for a product, you exponentially increase the growth potential of your business.

Once your funnels are in place, send all your paid traffic, marketing efforts, email drops, *everything* to them. Remember, sales funnels convert at least THREE TIMES better than storefronts. Why bother spending any money sending traffic to your storefront? It makes more sense to channel all paid marketing efforts to the dedicated funnels that provide the most profitable return on your marketing dollars.

What About My Store?

At this point, you're probably wondering why you should even bother having a store when you can make so much more money with funnels. Some people follow that logic and completely scrap their storefronts. I have friends with multi-million dollar businesses that rely solely on funnels and have no storefronts at all.

You could get rid of your store if you like, but I don't think it's a good idea. Instead, supplementing a storefront with funnels is the best long-term approach.

I would let your store get all its traffic from your back-end marketing to existing customers and let prospective customers find your store through organic sources such as press releases, blog posts, and search engines. Send all customer acquisition traffic to your funnels. Once a customer buys your products through one of your funnels and starts to trust your company, you can send them to your storefront via email to make repeat purchases. Plus, when they buy from the store, they still have upsell paths that are activated based on the products they purchase.

A storefront also gives your business some added credibility. If your customers Google you and find your store, they believe that your company is credible and professional. It also makes it easier for your customers to spread the word about your business; they can send their friends a link to the awesome product they bought through your store.

Conclusion

Sales funnels have **revolutionized** the way I do business. Without focusing on funnels in my ecommerce businesses, I would not have reached my level of success. I have yet to see this method fail to convert more than a storefront.

Some of my students and Mastermind members were skeptical about funnels because they seem too complicated and time consuming, but I'll tell you the same thing I told them: All it takes to start is ONE funnel for ONE product. Once you see the success of that one funnel, I promise you'll wonder how you ever survived without them.

Chapter 1 Summary

Funnel-based ecommerce on average converts 3 to 5 percent higher on the front end than a storefront and can increase your average order value by as much as 60 percent.

There are two types of ecom funnels: the stand-alone funnel and the upsell funnel path. Your business should use both. Within upsell funnel paths, there are three subtypes (default upsell funnel path, product-specific upsell funnel path, and behavior-based upsells); the type you use depends on what your ecommerce platform supports.

All active marketing and promotion efforts should be aimed at a stand-alone sales funnel, never at your storefront. Incorporate sales funnels into your business by creating dedicated funnels for each of your products, starting with the best-selling item.

CHAPTER 2

RECURRING INCOME CORE

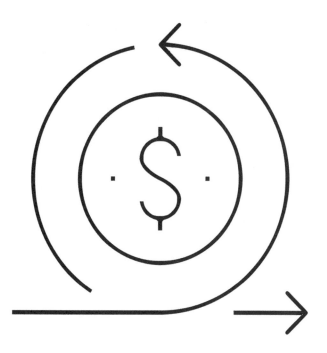

Not all revenue is created equal. Yes, a dollar earned is a dollar earned, but the more predictable that dollar is–the more likely you are to receive that dollar on a regular basis–the more valuable it is to your business. This is called **recurring income**.

Recurring income is *revenue earned on a residual or automated basis after the first sale*. This occurs at weekly, monthly, biannual, or any other scheduled increment.

This income is incredibly valuable to a business due to its predictable nature, but the majority of ecommerce companies don't understand or think about it at all. They are so focused on individual sales that they don't consider anything else. The companies that go against the grain and master recurring income, however, are the ones that experience the greatest growth and profitability.

The Power of Recurring Income

In Principle 12, you learned that one of the three ways to grow your business is to increase purchase frequency. Recurring revenue does just that. The sale comes in, not just once, but many times.

When you have recurring income, every time you bill, you get another purchase. Your company can depend on the baseline income derived from recurring income every month (or week or whatever increment of time), which goes a long way towards building a high cash flow business. Additionally, recurring income generates more money out of the exact same customers instead of forcing you to rely solely on new customers.

For the longest time, in the ecommerce space, recurring income was the secret of the supplement industry. These companies realized early on that because their products are consumable, they could automate regular transactions. They could charge customers a recurring fee and ship their products automatically each month.

Supplement companies did this well years before everyone else caught on, enabling them to build some of the biggest ecommerce companies in the world. These huge supplement companies are typically much more profitable than other businesses, and it's not because the supplement market is more profitable. It's because of that nice, reliable recurring income.

Most ecommerce businesses don't take advantage of recurring income because they don't consider themselves subscription businesses. Instead, they focus on one-time sales. In my years of experience with thousands of students, coaching clients, and Mastermind members, I have learned that this approach is **flawed and ultimately deadly for your business**.

In the near future, I believe ecommerce businesses that don't incorporate some form recurring revenue will really struggle to stay afloat. So you'd better get on the bandwagon now, because trust me, you'll be hurting later if you don't.

Recurring Income as the Focal Point of Your Business

I firmly believe that recurring income should be *the focal point of your entire business*. That's why I called it a RIC...Recurring Income CORE, i.e. the "core" of your business. If you don't have some form of a RIC in your business, it's time for a change, you need to restructure your business–from the ground up if necessary–to focus on recurring income.

If you agree to make that change, prepare for the growing pains of adjustment. In the long run, however, you'll wonder how your business ever survived without a recurring income core. Your company will stabilize, cash flow will improve, profits will grow, and your business will be much less stressful.

This is *critical* for a sustainable business. You don't go into the ecommerce business hoping to make money today and not tomorrow–you get into this business so that you don't have to have a job, so that you can work for yourself, take care of your family, and hopefully have lots of time off. If your business is not sustainable, you don't have any of that.

Of course, it's easier said than done and I understand what a big undertaking it is, but I also practice what I preach and I wouldn't tell you to do it if I hadn't already done it with great success. I have three main ecommerce brands, and they all are **100 percent focused on continuity and recurring income**. That is not to say that they only sell continuity offers, but rather that all sales of our regular physical products ultimately lead to getting people to join our subscription programs. The goal of everything I do in those businesses is to funnel customers into one of my monthly billing products because that's where the real profits are.

65 percent of my profits in those businesses comes from recurring income. Every month, 65 percent of my profits are already accounted for, and I know it will continue to grow. My recurring income compounds and gets bigger and bigger every month.

I used to have equity stakes in other brands, and I gave up my stake in any of the companies that wouldn't adapt to a recurring income core for their business. I did this because I knew I could make *ten or twenty times more money* focusing on businesses that build recurring income using physical products.

I'm not the only one doing this. Actress Jessica Alba's business, Honest Company, focuses on recurring income too, and her company was recently estimated to be worth over $1.7 billion.[10] It sells all kinds traditional ecommerce products to people around the world.

---

[10] http://fortune.com/2015/08/14/jessica-alba-honest-valuation/

Honest Company completely revolves around a monthly subscription and makes automatic monthly deliveries of essentials like soap, diapers, and feminine products. While a customer is free to make single purchases from the storefront, the entire business is structured to funnel people into one of their subscription plans or recurring billing plans. Basically, Jessica Alba has built a company worth over a billion dollars doing exactly what I'm telling you to do.

Still not convinced? Here are some of the best reasons why incorporating a recurring income core is an absolute must for your business.

Predictable Income

Ecom businesses are usually cash poor. They have all their money tied up in advertising, inventory, raw materials, and overhead. It's not at all uncommon for an ecom businesses to earn a million or more dollars per month and have less than $20,000 in the bank.

Additionally, most ecom businesses have totally unpredictable income. Ecommerce business earnings, when charted, often look like a heart rate monitor. As long as your ups are bigger than your downs, overall you should do okay. But the dips can give business owners serious anxiety, and being cash poor limits business growth (see principles 7 and 10).

Recurring income helps with both of these issues by providing predictable income. It's a stable safety net for your business. You don't have as many peaks and valleys, and when you do get some variation, you know you can count on your recurring income core to keep you afloat.

RICs have the added benefit of making businesses more recession proof. The market and economy goes up and down, but when you have recurring revenue, your business is stable and therefore not as susceptible to an unpredictable marketplace change.

To illustrate just how beneficial this can be, let's examine two hypothetical ecommerce businesses that are each doing about $50,000 a month in revenue. Business #1 is a traditional ecommerce business with no recurring revenue. In the first month, it makes $50,000. At the start of second month, it's at $0. *Every single month*, Business #1 has to start over and get back to where they were the previous month. That's not a good place to be as a business owner.

Business #2 also makes $50,000 a month, but makes 50 percent of its income from recurring revenue. At the end of the first month, they've made $50,000 in revenue. At the beginning of the second month, because 50 percent of their incomes from recurring income, they are GUARANTEED $25,000 of income.

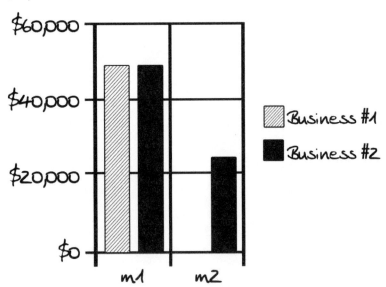

Business #2 doesn't have to start over from zero–it has a baseline income no matter what. That makes a huge difference, especially in times of economic turmoil. Now ask yourself: Would you rather own Business #1 or Business #2?

Compound Growth Effect

With recurring revenue, every new member *increases the monthly total of your recurring income stream.* This produces great compound growth for your monthly income.

Let's say you add 25 people to your recurring revenue program every week. At the end of one month, that's 100 people. If those people are each paying $50 a month, you now have $5,000 in monthly recurring revenue.

The next month you get 100 new recurring revenue customers, and at the end of the second month, your monthly recurring revenue is $10,000.

After one year, you have 1,200 members in your recurring revenue program and a monthly recurring revenue of $60,000 a month–and that's with a basic, unimpressive growth rate!

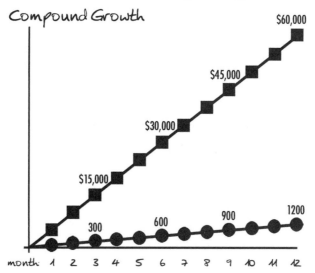

This is a simple example, but it shows exactly how effective a recurring income core is. Your monthly recurring revenue grows at a compounded rate as long as you continue acquiring new members at a faster rate than you lose them.

Obviously not every customer can stay with your business forever; we've all cancelled a monthly subscription before. But as long as you bring in customers faster than you lose them, you enjoy a snowball effect in your monthly income.

Types, Styles, and Frequencies of Recurring Income Cores

When I discuss recurring income cores in talks and seminars, many people say it's a great idea, but they also say they have no clue how it could work in their business. Others say they don't think they can make a recurring income core work for their particular niche. Perhaps you're thinking the same thing right now.

Remember Principle 1? Your business is not unique! Whether it's one of the styles or a combination of them, there IS a continuity plan that will work for your business, no matter what kind of product you sell. This section reveals some of the major types of continuity cores and how they work.

Types of Recurring Income Cores

Now that you understand what a recurring income core is and what it could do for your business, let's explore the various types of recurring income cores that you can add to your ecom business. Many of these RIC types can be used individually, but they can also be mixed and matched to maximize your profit and fit the needs and wants of your customers.

Consumable Subscriptions

This is by far the most common type of recurring income. Amazon, for instance, has great consumable subscription programs that delivers toilet paper, diapers, wipes, food, and other products. You can easily do this too.

Let's say you own a supplement brand that sells fish oil pills, and each bottle contains a one-month supply. After a customer makes their first purchase, you can offer to deliver more fish oil pills to the customer every month automatically. When they sign up for the subscription program, customers typically get better pricing because they agreed to automatic monthly shipments.

If any of the products you sell or plan to sell in your store have a consumable nature, then offering them an auto-ship subscription plan is a no brainer. People love convenience and anything that makes their life easier.

Subscription Box

A subscription box is a collection of physical products that is shipped to customers on a regular basis as part of a recurring billing program. With a subscription box, customers pay a flat fee for great value, convenience, and the fun of getting something in the mail every month. While subscription boxes are growing in popularity, they've been around for decades; anything that ends with "of the Month" (Wine of the Month, Cheese of the Month) qualifies as a subscription box.

Subscription boxes are great for niche businesses, especially businesses that don't have a consumable aspect but still want to ship out physical products. Almost any business can take a collection of their products and turn into a box and ship it out to people. There are subscription boxes for practically everything these days from Pokémon to gardening to sex toys, the sky's the limit when it comes to the types niches subscription boxes will work for.

Two great examples of new-wave subscription boxes are BarkBox and Birchbox. BarkBox is for dog owners. The customer chooses a BarkBox for a small, medium, or large dog and receives a dog treat, a toy, and other dog products each month.[11] Birchbox, which started in 2010, sends deluxe makeup and beauty samples each month for $10. If a customer likes one of the samples, they get a discount on the full-size item.[12]

Some subscription boxes nowadays charge a flat fee, but include a prepaid envelope so customers can return items they don't like. Many clothing subscription box companies use this model. It can be more volatile than a typical recurring income core, though, because you don't know what your customers will actually keep. Yes, you keep the flat fee, but that fee is nominal when you consider shipping costs, your profits come only when the customer chooses to keep the items in the box. The unpredictable nature of this type of continuity program makes it my least favorite option for a RIC.

Digital

Digital memberships are typically information based. They don't require fulfillment through the mail and there's little to no product cost, so digital subscriptions have a high profit margin–typically around 80 to 90 percent. Traditional

---

[11] https://www.barkbox.com/

[12] https://www.birchbox.com/

membership sites that offer access to videos, written content, or a community forum fall under this category, but so do new, out of the box models.

Digital subscriptions work for practically any business. For example, a fitness business that sells exercise equipment could offer a digital membership that provides access to nutrition advice, stretching routines and workouts involving the products it sells. A car stereo or accessories brand could sell how-to videos, installation tips, insider looks at the latest-and-greatest technology, and more. The possibilities are endless.

Newsletters (Physical or Digital)

Any business can sell a newsletter, but I've found that newsletters work best in passion-based niches. A general or regular electronics retailer probably won't get people to sign up for a paid newsletter, but a downhill mountain biking retailer has passionate customers who are more likely to buy a newsletter subscription that caters to their passions.

I have newsletters for two of my businesses, and I send them on no less than a quarterly basis. Most businesses choose to offer them every month or every other month; I prefer monthly because that way, you can bill your customers more often and it keeps you on their mind which is great for boosting the likelihood of repeat purchases.

You can even market your products in your newsletters. Just include articles about the latest and greatest items, direct your customers to your store to buy, and offer coupon codes. Newsletters also work great as an add on to a different type of RIC as a way of boosting the perceived value to make it easier to justify your price.

Buyer's Clubs

Buyer's clubs are another easy form of recurring income. A buyer's club is an elite customer level that someone can join for a monthly, quarterly, or annual fee in exchange for perks such as free shipping or a flat-rate discount. The best example of an ecommerce buyer's club is Amazon Prime: Prime members get free two-day shipping, free movies, ebooks, and access to exclusive sales.

Many businesses with large buyer's clubs can also negotiate discounts with popular brands. These discount clubs offer special prices for customers even outside of your store. For instance, Costco (the large brick-and-mortar buyer's club) solicits discounts from resorts, popular events, movie theaters, and more.

Monthly buyer's clubs tend to work best at lower price points. Remember that Amazon Prime is only a little over a one hundred dollars per year. Buyer's clubs need to be seen as a no brainer offer with clearly defined benefits for the member that will enhance their experience with your brand.

Associations

There are many associations that have transitioned well to the internet, such as AAA or AARP. These credible associations have inspired the creation of thousands of new associations. Put simply, associations are the new "membership" for the online space.

Associations are similar to newsletters in that they work well in passion niches, for example if you sold products to people who owned Pit Bulls, then you could create the American Pit Bull Owners Association and you would find that a portion of your customers would gladly join it. Now I have no idea if the APBOA is a real association, but I can guarantee you there is something like it out there in practically every passion market you can find, because people want to belong—they want to be a part of something. Associations are the perfect solution to this need, and the more strongly they believe in the topic, the more likely they will be to join. They'll pay to join, and you grant them access to your association and whatever benefits you choose to offer. Take a minute and google a few different associations and see what they are giving their members. Many of them are nothing more than a private forum, a periodic newsletter and possibly a membership card.

I've started several associations that are affiliated with my various businesses. It's easy to do—just create your own association with a .org domain and a title that fits your niche. You can combine an association with some of the other types of recurring income cores. For example, a membership to your association could be a perk for customers when they join your subscription box or buyer's club.

Micro Continuity

Micro continuity is the last topic in this section because it can be applied to nearly any type of recurring income core. You could have a micro-continuity digital newsletter or a micro-continuity subscription box, for example. It's so easy to apply because micro continuity memberships cost less than $10 per month (thus the name).

Micro-continuity pricing is set at impulse purchase prices that customers don't have to give any thought to buying. One of the best price points for micro continuity is $4.95 because that's low enough to encourage impulse purchases, and it's effortless to provide value for such a small price.

Lots of people go through their credit statements like hawks, and they seldom complain about a $4.95 charge. No matter how simple canceling your service is, it's still a hassle for the customer. More often than not, the customer won't bother canceling such a small monthly fee.

I use micro-continuities a lot. One example was a micro-continuity weekly email newsletter I used to run in the Second Amendment niche called the Armed Citizen. This was it consisted of:

- **Week one**: An article on a random second-amendment topic

- **Week two**: An article written by an expert exclusively for our newsletter

- **Week three:** A discount or a special offer from a popular brand (exclusively for our subscribers)

- **Week four**: Information on what happened in the Second Amendment world in the past month

The Armed Citizen has no fulfillment cost because it was a digital subscription, and the newsletter itself cost a little over $1,500 a month to outsource the writing and production. We ran the email newsletter for three years and made a ridiculous ROI, all from $4.95 a month from our customers. We ultimately combined the Armed Citizen newsletter with one of our associations and merged the two subscriptions.

Choosing RIC Types

A lot of these RIC types can be mixed and matched as I mentioned previously, and they *should* be mixed and matched to provide the most unbeatable value for your customers. For example, you can combine a buyer's club with a subscription box so that each time a customer joins your subscription box, they also get perks like free shipping or a 10 percent discount on every order. Alternatively, you can combine an association and a newsletter to create a higher value—and justify a higher price. Use whatever combination you want to create the best RIC for your niche.

Which recurring income core types might work for your business? Circle all that apply.

- Consumable subscription

- Subscription Box

- Digital

- Newsletter (physical or digital)

- Buyer's club

- Associations

- Micro continuity

Styles of Recurring Income Core

There are three styles of recurring income core: subscription, membership, and a hybrid model that combines the first two styles. Both memberships and subscriptions are useful, and there's a lot of material on the difference between these two styles.

I believe the hybrid model, which compounds the strengths of both styles, is generally the best choice for ecom businesses.

I'll explain subscription and membership styles below so you'll get why I prefer using a hybrid model.

Subscription

Subscriptions (consumable auto-ship programs, subscription boxes, and newsletters) are the least involved style of RIC. They involve very little interaction between the business and the customer. It's a straight product for money type relationship

Subscriptions provide dollar value, but do nothing to build intrinsic or relational value that fosters that sense of brand loyalty and helps to build a loyal following. This doesn't mean subscriptions aren't a good idea, but they should be viewed simply as a way to earn money. If you are also looking to build a tribe of brand loyal passionate customers, you'll need to take some additional steps.

Membership

Memberships (associations, buyer's clubs, and digital memberships) are more about the brand than subscriptions are. Whenever you deliver content instead of just products, you are providing personality, intrinsic value, and something people can identify with in addition to dollar value.

Memberships build a tribe of customers that likes your products and your Brand and what it stands for. There's dollar value to a membership, and there's also a sense of belonging that makes it harder for members want to cancel. Because these fans are loyal, memberships typically have a higher retention rate than subscription businesses do. For the vast majority of the population, dollar value is less important than intrinsic or non-tangible value.

Hybrid

I believe that if you combine subscriptions and memberships, you wind up with a much more successful continuity than either style could provide on its own. As you may remember from Principle 8, you need to be brand centric, not product centric. Mixing the two styles creates more loyal customers and money while generating longer retention rates and more satisfied customers. Ultimately, the hybrid model creates brand ambassadors who tell everyone about your business, and that's something every business needs.

No matter how you decide to combine subscriptions and memberships, if you decide to go this route, your hybrid model should create amazing value that customers can't say "no" to. The customers need to feel like they are getting MORE value (both intrinsic and dollar) than what they are paying for so they don't want to quit.

I created my own style of hybrid by mixing physical subscriptions with digital memberships. In one of my businesses, I do a combination subscription box (stuff in the mail every month) and digital memberships (a monthly newsletter, access to a members-only online community, and a buyer's club that offers discounts). I satisfy ALL my customers' needs by providing something physical every month in addition to an emotionally fulfilling community.

Frequencies

Daily, weekly, monthly, quarterly, and annually billing frequencies are all used for RICs, along with lots of combinations thereof (such as bimonthly). However, monthly, quarterly, and annual billing are the most common by far.

I prefer monthly billing because it provides the most predictable cash flow, and I recommend building your programs around monthly billing unless there's some unique reason why it wouldn't work for your business. However, if you choose to bill monthly or at a larger time increment, remember that *the more infrequently you bill, the larger the price point should be*. The amount you bill should also include a discount after you add up the total of all the months they are paying for in advance (this makes the subscription worth it to the customer).

Adding a Recurring Income Core to Your Business

After making an informed decision about which RIC style or model to use, the next step is to 1) implement it and 2) figure out how to get your customers to buy it.

Your initial conversion rate may not be phenomenal when you first roll out your RIC in your business, but remember: this is about long-term growth. Even if a small percentage of your customers buy your RIC, the recurring charges still add up and compound every single month. If you're anywhere above a 10 percent conversion rate of people joining your RIC, you're doing pretty well.

Across my businesses, I have about a 16 percent global average. In some of my businesses, I have as high as 20 or 25 percent, and I work hard to increase it even when it's that high. However, we've found after doing this for years on end that it's fairly easy to make big increases in your RIC conversion rate up until you get around 30%. When you start trying to optimize to convert higher than 30% you will start seeing marginal gains for much more time and effort than it is probably worth. When you make it to this point, congratulations, stop trying to optimize and instead spend that time boosting your acquisition of front end customers.

Technology

Before adding recurring revenue to your business, *make sure you have the technology in place to handle it.* Your technology needs to automatically handle recurring billing, trial offers, upgrades, cancellations, pausing, restarting, and fulfillment management. You also need to make sure your ecommerce platform supports the way you plan on selling your RIC.

Most of the major ecommerce platforms have these functionalities either built in or available as add-on app or upgrade. If your platform does not support these features, it'll probably limit your business in the long run and you need to think seriously about migrating to a more robust platform.

Believe me, it'll be easier now than later, when your business is larger. Once you have the proper technology in place, you can leverage the added functionality to rapidly scale.

Selling Your RIC

It's no secret that continuity is a hard sell on the front end. It's hard to get a new customer who doesn't know or trust you to agree to monthly billing; it's much easier to sell them a one-time product. This means business owners have to be a little bit sneaky when selling their RIC. There are two main avenues that work well for this.

Upsells

The sales funnels you learned about in Chapter 1 are an awesome way to snag new RIC customers. I teach all my coaching students to set up their RIC behind every static product they sell as an upsell path.

No matter what product customers purchase in your store, *the first or second upsell (depending on how your funnel path flows) should be your Recurring Income Core.* Subscription revenue should be the focal point of your business, so it should be your default upsell offer and it should be built into your stand-alone sales funnels the same way.

Trials

Getting people to give your RIC a chance and try it out can be tough. This is where a 'trial' offer can be a huge help. A Discount trial lowers the cost of the first month so that the customer can 'test the waters' with less risk and actually experience what you're offering, then if they enjoy it, chances are they'll stick with it.

I have a $29 monthly continuity in my Second Amendment niche business, and I offer a $1 trial for the first month as the default upsell in all of our stand alone funnels and upsell paths. We currently have a seven-month retention rate for people who take the trial. Meaning that as long as we can get a customer to give our RIC a shot, the vast majority will stay part of the program for at least 7 months. Most subscription programs have a three to four-month retention rate, so for us to have a 7-month retention rate means our customers are VERY satisfied and we're working everyday to increase our retention rate even more. Because we offer the first month for $1 we actually lose money on their first month's membership.

It takes us two months to break even on the $1 trial, but because our retention rate is seven months, it's worth it. It takes time to determine your retention rate and locate your member drop-off points (if you've only had your trial offer for a month, there's no way of knowing), but over time you'll figure out what it is and then you can use what you learn in the retention management section below to get them to stay longer.

Trial offers can also be used to make sales directly on the front end–just plant the offer in your store as a product or send an autoresponder email promo campaign stating that you're running a special. For example, you can send a customer an email saying, "Hey, our Second Amendment subscription box is usually $29 a month, but because you are a new customer we want to say thank you by offering you a one-time chance to get the first month for only $1." After the first month, continue to bill the customer at the regular rate and start raking in the profits.

Multiple Continuity Streams

A single RIC program should be the focal point of your business, but once it's in place, it's okay to leverage another one. Multiple levels of the same RIC work in a single business, and so can multiple different types of RICs.

Create one RIC offer, and then if more levels with different price points make sense for your business, add them. A lot of subscription boxes do that; they let customers spend more money to get more stuff.

My Second Amendment business has two continuity programs: a $29 monthly RIC and a $4.95 per month micro continuity association. We have two different continuity programs within the same business, and we offer them to customers at different times. Some customers buy both, but others who support the cause but are sensitive to higher price points only purchase the micro continuity.

The association takes more customer volume to make as much money as the subscription, but every new member to either program adds to the total recurring revenue stream. We try to get customers to move from one to both, but either way our income continues to compound and grow every single month

Retention Management

Once you have customers in your RIC, the goal is to keep them in your program. A study by Bain and Company shows that even a 5 percent increase in customer retention can lead to a 25 to *95 percent increase in profits*,[13] and this compounds when you factor in recurring revenue and its effect on the lifetime value of a customer. That's a serious increase—one that could completely change your business.

While it's definitely worth the effort, a recurring revenue program is different from traditional ecommerce and requires some additional work on your part. An RIC is an *ongoing agreement between you and the customer* and it brings added responsibilities that you're probably not used to.

It's kind of like being in a relationship. You have obligations to fulfill to your customer—delivering product, content, access on a regular basis, whatever it is you promised in exchange for regular payments. You need to provide value

---

[13] http://hbswk.hbs.edu/archive/1590.html

and keep the customer happy, engaged, and loyal because the longer they stay a member, the more money you make. Additionally, the happier you keep them, the more likely they are to become brand ambassadors who spread the word about your company.

The 10x Rule

The 10x Rule is my overriding rule for retention management (and sales in general): **Always provide ten times the perceived value of what you charge**. This has become the standard in the information marketing space, but is often overlooked in the physical product world. If you can provide 10 times the perceived value for whatever your customers are paying, you'll have a much happier customer base and a more successful continuity program.

Did you notice the word "perceived" in that definition? That is important. *The perceived value of your RIC doesn't have to be a hard dollar value.* If they're paying $10, you shouldn't send them a $100 product. It's all about the customer's perception of the product.

Take Amazon Prime, for example. It costs $100 for a membership, but most Prime members think they're getting more than ten times the value of what they pay. That's not dollar-for-dollar value; it's all perks and benefits that add up to a much higher 'perceived value'.

This is why my businesses use hybrid model RIC's. If you combine information with your physical products (a newsletter, a buyer's club loyalty program, whatever), you significantly increase perceived value without incurring much, if any additional expense. It's a win-win for everyone.

Retention Metrics

In ecommerce, there are tons of metrics and Key Performance Indicators (KPIs) you should be tracking to better understand your business. There's a whole bunch of new metrics just for subscriptions as well, but for retention management, there are only three that matter.

1. Churn Rate (CR)

The churn rate is a short-term metric that shows what percentage of customers cancel their subscriptions in a given time period. My companies, for instance, lose an average of 12 percent of their customer base per month. The lower the churn rate, the better your membership.

Churn rate should be calculated on a regular basis. You should keep track of what your churn rate is for customers who have been with you for different points of time. I.e. customers who have been a part of your RIC for 2 months may have a 18% churn rate, but customers who are in their third month only have 11% churn rate. Knowing this data will help you improve the retention rates of your RIC.

To calculate your churn rate, use the following equation:

Churn Rate

$$\text{Churn} = \frac{\text{Customers Lost During Date Range}}{\text{Customers At Beginning Of Date Range}}$$

2. Customer Count Retention (CCR)

Customer count retention is only calculable for RICs that have existed for a while, because you need data for a significant length of time to make the calculation worthwhile. If you've had your continuity program for a year, how many of the original customers remain active a year later? If your program has only been around for three months or six months, you have to measure it for that time frame.

All RICs have an average length of time that people remain members, but that is just the 'average'. What about the customers who don't drop off, how long do they stay? 6 months? 9 months? One year? Customer count retention tells you this and calculating it is as simple as running a report in your CRM for customers who have been part of that specific program for a specific date range.

3. Average Subscription Revenue Per Customer (ASRC)

The average subscription revenue is separate from the lifetime value of your customer, which includes both RIC and one-time purchase income. Do not confuse the two. Your average subscription revenue shows how much you earn from a customer in your RIC program. In other words, how much on average does a customer spend before they cancel their subscription?

This metric gives you a good idea of the success of your program. It's important because it reveals how much money you can afford to spend to keep customers and still be profitable.

To calculate your average subscription revenue per customer, use the following equation:

Average Subscription Revenue Per Customer

$$ASRC = \frac{RIC}{Price} \times \begin{array}{c} Avg\ RIC \\ Retention \\ Rate \end{array}$$

If you offer a 1-month Trial to your RIC, then your calculation would look like:

ASRC with 1 month trial

$$ASRC = \frac{RIC\ Trial}{Price} + \left(\frac{RIC}{Price} \times \left(\begin{array}{c} Avg\ RIC \\ Retention \\ Rate \end{array} - \frac{Trial}{Month} \right) \right)$$

Typically, average subscription revenue is consistent; if a customer stays for four months and pays $20 per month, they spend $80. It's a standardized number. There may be variations if you have multiple price points to your memberships, but in that case then you should calculate statistics for your levels of memberships separately because they each attract a different type of customer.

Drop-Off Points

After you've calculated these three metrics, it's time to find the drop-off points in your RIC memberships. A drop-off point is basically a billing period in your RIC where an abnormally high number of people cancel. They are simple to calculate and they tie in with the individual month churn rate calculations you learned above. To determine your drop-off points, make a chart or graph (like the one below) that depicts the churn rate for customers at each point (month) in your RIC.

Dropoff Points

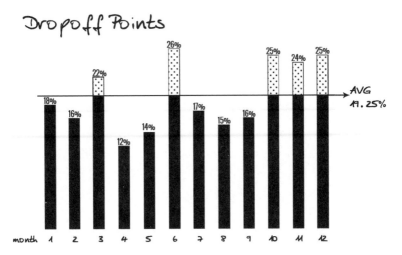

The figure above shows Churn Rates for 12 months of a RIC. In this example the Average churn rate for the year is 19.25% which is just slightly higher than the subscription industry average of 18%, so it's not bad. But you can also notice that there are several months (3,6,10,11,12) that are higher than the average. These are the main (above average) drop-off points for this RIC.

The members who stay past those drop-off points (three months, six months, whatever) are your most loyal customers. If you have a three-month retention rate, customers that make it past the three-month mark will likely stay with you (at least until your next big drop-off point).

You'll start to notice drop-off points a few months after launching your RIC. When you do, try to figure out *why* customers are dropping off at that point. Is it because the product is the same every month? Is there no value? Whatever the problem is, you NEED to fix it.

One of the most effective ways to do that is to create what we call a 'retention booster' at the drop-off point. If customers drop off on the third month, automatically offer them a bonus, incentive, or some kind of extra perk for that third month. Tell your customers about the new perk towards the end of the second month and let them know it's coming soon. Deliver the perk after they are charged for their third month of subscription so they'll want to stick around.

Use Retention Boosters at every drop-off point you find in your business to dramatically increase both the Average Subscription Revenue Per Customer (ASRC) and your overall Lifetime Customer Value (LTV).

I have successfully done this in my businesses for years, and it's made a HUGE difference in my bottom line. In my Second Amendment business, we found that 20 percent of our RIC customers were canceling in the fourth month, so we checked to see what was wrong with our month 4 subscription box. What made our customers cancel before they even saw what we were offering in the fifth month?

By calling a bunch of the customers who cancelled, we discovered that we were sending shotgun cleaning kits in this particular box. The problem was the products weren't universal, so if the customer didn't have a shotgun, they weren't excited to receive the products in the box. We swapped out the cleaning kit for a cool tactical rifle sling that can be used on any long gun, and it cut our cancellation rate in the fourth month from 20 to 11 percent.

Even after we made that change, we noticed that the 4th month still had a higher drop-off rate than any of the next 3 months. At that point, we realized that our customers were not feeling appreciated. So before the rebill for fifth month, we sent our customers an email thanking them for being a valued member for four months and offering to include a free pocketknife in their next box. Of course, the next box was shipped right after their billing date for the next month. Once we did that, our fourth month churn rate dropped to only 3 percent, an 8 percent reduction that only added $5 (cost of knife) to the cost per user for that month.

Our next big drop-off point was in the seventh month of membership. Because the customer has been subscribed for over half a year at that point, we decided to try something new. At the seventh month, we offer our customers an option to upgrade to an annual payment in exchange for a discount. If they pay for the rest of the year (five months), they get a 10 percent discount; if they pay for a whole new year, they get a 20 percent discount.

This has been so effective that we're testing it right now in other niches. It works because if they don't want a discounted annual plan, chances are they were going to cancel anyway. If we get a percentage of those people to take the offer, we multiplying our money. We weren't going to get that customer for more than four to six months, and now we have them for a whole year with only a slight reduction in profit.

If you have a digital membership without a physical cost, it's easy to offer customers a lifetime upgrade. In my experience, this works way better than an annual subscription for several reasons. First, it doesn't cost the business anything and the take rate is significantly higher. Second, if you get customer on a lifetime digital membership, you get a customer for life. They will always receive your digital product, newsletter, emails and the like, which should include all kinds of special offers and discounts to your other physical products.

Make Canceling Simple, But Not Painless

There are plenty of ecom platforms that offer a one-click cancel link in an email or in their members' area–all the customer has to do is click a button and their subscription is over. I'm big on providing good customer service, but at the same time, you're in business to make money. Don't shoot yourself in the foot by making canceling your continuity program too easy.

This is especially important if you're shipping physical products. Let's say you shipped your product on Monday and they clicked cancel on Tuesday. Guess what? The customer will blow up your customers support when they get the product AFTER they canceled, this usually leads to a refund request or a chargeback. And most won't want to ship your product back to you. You've just lost all the money on the stuff you shipped and created a customer's support nightmare.

In all our businesses, customers have to call our customer support phone number to cancel. We do this for three reasons:

1. The extra work makes the customer think twice about canceling and wonder if it's worth the effort.
2. When they cancel via phone or email, you can ask them why they're canceling. A majority give you a poor excuse, but some people give you something you can fix.
3. You can try to change their mind if they contact you. Give them a free month, a 50 percent discount, or some other incentive for them to stay. You'll save a percentage of those sales, I guarantee you, and any member you keep helps compound returns on your overall income.

Conclusion

I hope this chapter has convinced you that everything in your business absolutely needs to revolve around recurring income core. Think of it like a bicycle wheel: the center section is the RIC and the spokes (your other physical products) support it. As long as the structure is sound, the wheel works perfectly. A RIC provides financial stability for your business, and what business owner doesn't want that?

A recurring income core should be *the most consistent profit center of your entire business*. That's why it should be a standard upsell behind every single product you sell. If you focus on making a recurring income core upsell or downsell–or however you're positioning it–you'll never end up with a flat tire on your business. I don't stress out about where the money is coming from in a business with a recurring revenue core; with an RIC, I know I make more money every day regardless of what happens out in the market or on the front end.

Chapter 2 Summary

Recurring income is income that comes in on a residual or automated basis. It can be collected weekly, monthly, biannually, or any other increment of your choice, but monthly is best for most ecom businesses.

We call it a Recurring Income Core (RIC) because subscription revenue should form the CORE of your ecommerce business and all other products you sell should feed into it.

There are two styles of recurring income cores: subscription (consumable subscriptions, subscription boxes, and newsletters) and memberships (digital, buyer's club, and associations). A hybrid of subscription and membership RICs provides the benefits of both styles.

When adding a RIC to your business, first make sure the technology is in place, then incentivize customers with upsells and trials and use multiple continuity streams.

Retain RIC customers by following the 10X rule, tracking important metrics (churn rate, customer count retention, and average subscription revenue per client), finding and managing drop-off points, and making canceling a little bit painful.

CHAPTER 3

THINK BEFORE YOU SELL

You may spend lots of time on your logo or the colors you choose for your website, but you probably have not spent much time thinking about selling smart.

I know you are busy, but *you must have a thought process behind everything you do.* Successful ecommerce businesses do not just happen; they are 100% premeditated. You HAVE to know how to engineer your profit margins so that your prices can adequately support your business. You HAVE to know the difference between OEM and private label products, and know which one better suits your business. You HAVE to know how you can augment your business with additional income streams that don't negatively impact your already stretched cash flow.

Most business owners gloss over all of this, but I don't want you to be like most business owners. We'll cover all of this and more in this chapter.

Product Pricing: It's All About the Margin

I want to talk about margins first because they play a huge role in the products you can (and should) offer. A profit margin is the difference between how much you sell your product for and how much it actually costs. The higher the profit margin in your business is, the easier it is for your ecommerce business to grow and profit.

Most businesses give their margins only a passing thought, and those that do care about their margins often do not do the math correctly. A lot of people think that if their product costs $25 and they sell it for $50, their profit is $25 and that's the number they tell everyone and use when they try to operate their business. The math is technically correct, but using that math is what causes many ecommerce businesses to fail. If someone with those numbers actually calculated their customer acquisition as well as other fixed expenses, and factored that in, they may discover that they have a negative margin. There are tons of business owners who have *no idea* they have a negative margin, which is a very dangerous position to be in.

One of the reasons people do not know their true margin is because, as I mentioned in the Core Principles section, most business owners have no formal business training. The resources available online are usually so boring that many people prefer not to learn, or they skip over this topic completely. Furthermore, most small businesses don't have any real C-level executives, much less a Chief Financial Officer (CFO) whose job it is to calculate and interpret this type of data.

Let's break the cycle now and make sure you are not someone whose business gets bitten by 'margin'. There are three types of profit margins you should be aware of:

1. **Gross Profit Margin**: At a unit level, the gross profit margin is the sales price of that unit minus the cost of goods sold. To calculate it, deduct your sales prices from the cost of actually producing and manufacturing the product, but do not factor in the cost of shipping or selling the product. This is the basic profit margin that everyone talks about, and it's an important one to keep track of when you are sourcing and pricing products, but beyond that you don't really use it.

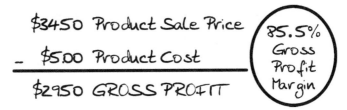

2. **Operating Profit Margin**: The most important margin, the heartbeat of your company, is your operating profit margin. It's also known as EBITDA, or "Earnings Before Interest, Taxes, Depreciation, and Amortization" in big business circles. Because it factors in more expenses, the operating profit margin says

more about your actual profits than the gross profit margin. There are two ways you can calculate it:

a. The operating profit margin can be calculated on a product level. This is the sales price of the product minus all fixed and variable costs associated with the product. To figure this number, find out how much of your operating expense is factored into a single product, then find out how much it costs to manufacture, sell, and fulfill one of those products. Add those 2 numbers together then take that total and subtract it by the sales price of the product. This will give you your Operating Profit Per Unit.

b. On a company level, operating profit margin is total sales volume minus everything it costs you to do business, excluding taxes and interest on debt. This is your basic "profit" that can be used to grow your business.

$3450 Product Sale Price
- $500 Product Cost
- $950 Operating Costs
_____
$2000 OPERATING PROFIT

58.0% Operating Profit Margin

3. **Net Profit Margin**: This margin, as you might have guessed, is sales revenue minus all costs, including taxes and interest on debt. This margin encompasses both of the above margins and reveals how much you're *really* making from the sale of each product. Net profit margin is important to look at on an annual basis, but not on a day-to-day basis, because your tax

ramifications do not emerge or get accurately classified on a daily basis.

$3450 Product Sale Price

- $500 Product Cost

- $950 Operating Costs

478% Net Profit Margin

- $350 Taxes/Debt Interest

$1650 NET PROFIT

Many people lump everything into either gross profit or net profit, but there's a big difference between the two. Gross profit margin is just the sales price minus the cost of goods sold, and net profit margin is a metric you can only calculate once a year because your tax liability changes on a daily basis as you buy and sell inventory.

Operating profit margin is the only usable metric for daily budgeting, forecasting, and the operation of your business, but you should calculate all three margins for the most comprehensive understanding of your profitability. Do the math and find out what it actually costs to sell your particular product and how much is actually left over. You'll more than likely be surprised by the answer, and you might want to make some changes as a result.

A study by MarketingSherpa shows that, on average, ecommerce businesses with gross revenues in the six-figure range have gross margins of **30 percent or less**,[14] and that 30 percent does not include any real expenses like advertising or overhead. If your cost of customer acquisition is 10 percent, as

---

[14] Burstein, D. (n.d.). Ecommerce Research Chart: Average gross margins for small, medium and large companies. Retrieved June 15, 2016, from https://www.marketingsherpa.com/article/chart/ecommerce-average-gross-margins

it often is in a business of this range, your margin goes down to 20 percent even BEFORE factoring other expenses like overhead, wages, fulfillment, and taxes. That's why it's *so important* to pay attention to more than just your gross profit margin.

The 3X Rule

A lot of companies that came from traditional retail either have keystone pricing or mark up every product by a flat, across-the-board mark up percentage (like 50 percent). The latter–marking up based on a whim instead of on facts–is a HUGE mistake.

I always remind myself–and tell my students to remember–that your margin is dictated by your markup (the difference between the price you sell your product for and how much it costs you to acquire it). When I calculate the markup for a new product, my basic rule of thumb is to mark it up *at least three times* its production value.

I call this the 3X rule, and here is what it comes down to: if you can't get 150 percent markup on your product, consider choosing a more lucrative product. I always follow the 3X rule–I won't sell a product unless I can mark it up at least three times the cost. If the product costs $5, I need to be able to sell it for at least $15. I have gotten so strict about it that I bypass a product completely if I cannot start at that markup, and often I will mark up a product even higher than that, but 3x is the bare minimum starting point.

The markup has to be that high because of your fixed and variable costs. Remember, you won't make $10 in profit on a $5 item. In my businesses, I typically wind up with around a 60 percent gross profit margin from a 150 percent markup. When I factor in another 20 percent for advertising and overhead, I wind up with a 40 percent operating profit margin. These are my ideal markup and margin numbers using the 3X rule:

- Markup: 150 percent
- Gross Profit Margin: 60 percent
- Operating Profit Margin: 40 percent
- Advertising and Overhead: 20 percent

When most ecommerce businesses say they have a 40 percent margin, they actually mean their gross profit margin (as per the MarketingSherpa study). When I say I have a 40 percent margin, I mean my operating margin. Because of that, I can spend more money on advertising and customer acquisition.

A final disclaimer: all I have talked about so far is percentages, but percentages are *not* all that matter when it comes to your profit margins. The actual dollar amount in the margin matters every bit as much as the percentage, if not more.

A 50 percent margin on a $10 product is not equal to a 50 percent margin on a $50 product. The $10 product only generates a $5 gross profit, whereas the $50 product generates a $25 gross profit. That's a pretty significant difference for products that both have a "50% margin", and it shows in a company's revenue and ability to scale.

What If the Product You Love Doesn't Meet the 3x Rule?

If you have a product you think is amazing, that you're passionate about, and it doesn't stand up to the 3X rule, know that you're not alone. While I sympathize with you (a little bit), when it comes down to it I DON'T CARE if your product is your life or how much you 'love' it. If you want to have a business, then have a business! Choose products that you can mark up enough to make a good profit.

In extenuating circumstances, there are some workarounds. If you have a product you're passionate about and the numbers don't work now, but they could work later if can get your economies of scale down, then consider these possibilities:

- Shelve the product for now and find another one in the same category with better profit potential. Use the alternate product to grow your business and customer base so that later, when you have both the finances and established customer base, you can support your investment in the initial product that you loved.

- Find a complementary product that can be sold alongside your main one. This product should sell as well or better than your main product and can be used to keep your business afloat and profitable. This leverages a concept known as a "Profit Maximizer," which will be discussed in detail in Chapter 4.

If your real goal is to build a successful business, you need to be able to put your product on the back burner no matter how much you want to sell it. If it's not ready to be sold or the numbers don't work, ask yourself: is it better to make NO profit on your existing product, or make money now with a different product, and sell your original product later?

Sell Your Own Products

Selling your own products means you have to shift away from the normal online retail philosophy and get rid of that monkey-see-monkey-do mentality. Don't be like everybody else! Don't start an online store that sells products that any of the other major retail juggernauts sell, because you'll be selling a 'commodity' not a product, and something your customer can probably buy from thousands of other stores for a lower price than you can afford to sell at.

A customer can buy a commoditized product at thousands of stores. If someone can buy the camcorder you sell for cheaper on Amazon, what compelling reason do they have to buy it from you?

You need to *give* people a reason to buy from your store. You have to convince people to buy from you by offering something worth buying, whether it is a private label product, an original product, or even a series of products in a brand of your own. You'll learn how to do exactly that in this section.

Don't Sell Sony

Even in niche markets, you are likely selling the same things everyone else is selling. Obviously a lot of stores do this, and some may be doing well, but you should *not* try to be like them. Here are just two compelling reasons why copying other retailers is a bad idea:

1. When you are a commoditized business, it's hard to get value out of products. If you ever want to sell your business, you'll discover that businesses with unique products are much more valuable. If you own the

brand, nobody else can sell it but you, and that means a lot when it comes time to sell.

2. When you sell branded products, you typically make a 20 to 40 percent gross profit, just like everyone else selling the same product. The more competitive the brand and its products, the more that margin gets squeezed, and the lower your actual profit. Name brand electronics have a pathetic 10 to 11 percent gross profit margin. When you sell your own products, on the other hand, you can control your prices and have products with a 60 percent or higher gross margin—*six times* the gross profit margin that most name-brand electronics sellers have.

All that being said, if you currently only offer other people's products, don't throw them all out! Instead, introduce a few of your own products to pad your overall profit margin while using your store to build your brand. Selling big-name products alongside your own gives your brand credibility by association—if you sell your brand's gadget next to similar Apple products, your customers are more likely to trust your brand even if they have never heard of it before.

One of my Black Label Mastermind members is in the electronics niche. When he came to me, his business was making $2 million a year and he had a 10 to 20 percent margin on most of the products in his store because they were all name brand electronics available all over the internet. He was not taking home a ton of money from his company, but he had been in business for 15 years and he thought that was just the way it was.

We worked with him to create his own line of products under his own brand. To do this we helped him figure out what was selling well in his store, worked with manufacturers in China to create his own versions with his branding, and sold these new products in his store alongside all the other name brand products he'd been selling for years. Without having to deal with a middleman (wholesaler), he was able to sell his own products for a lower price than the similar name-brand products, while maintaining a much higher profit margin. People started buying his products, and his yearly revenue jumped from $2 million to $3 million.

The point is, if you are afraid that creating your own brand of products is out of your league, fear not. We now live in a global economy where you can easily get ahold of manufacturers in Mexico, Sri Lanka, China, or any other country that manufactures the products you want. The costs associated with doing this are not nearly as high as you would think.

Product Selection and Manufacturer Selection Criteria

Before we get into how you can produce your own products, there are seven product selection criteria and two manufacturer selection criteria I want to share with you. Everything I sell meets these criteria, and I use these every time I look at adding a new product, evaluate an old product, or coach a student through the process of sourcing their own products.

Product Selection

1. **Niche specific**. Niche down and sell to a specific market (Principle 5). Your product needs to specifically fit and

cater to the niche market you've chosen to target. If it doesn't, then it's not the right product.

2. **Durable.** The more fragile your product is, the more likely it is to break, and broken products cannot be sold. It could break during shipping, either from your manufacturer to you or from you to your customer. It could also break in your warehouse or when the customer uses it for the first time.

   If your products have moving parts or electronics, a percentage of your products will be defective, and you'll need to account for it in advance and ensure that your profit margin can absorb that cost. Basically, the more shockproof and durable your product is, the better.

3. **Moderate to high quality**. The higher the quality of your product, the higher your customer satisfaction and the higher the price you can charge for it. I don't sell junk, and I do not recommend you sell junk. Anything marketed well enough can sell, but if you start with a moderate to high-quality product, you'll do a lot better with a lot less customer support headaches.

4. **In-demand.** Do people actually want the product? Maybe you saw it once in a movie and you thought it would be awesome to sell, but do people actually want it? This requires market research, and market research is worth its weight in gold. I would much rather know if people in my niche will buy my product before I spend $20,000 on inventory, wouldn't you?

5. **Retails for at least $25**. I won't touch a product that sells for less than $25. Anything sold for less has too low of a gross profit dollar amount, which will make it hard to operate and scale your business. A $10 product with a 50

percent gross margin means $5 in gross profit. This doesn't give you much money to work with and it requires you to sell a large volume of the product on a continual basis to generate any sizable profit that you could live on.

6. **Solid margins.** Your margins have to fit the type of business you run. Are you a high-end retailer or a bargain seller? If your product sells for at least $25, does it have solid margins that will provide you with enough operating profit to grow your business? In my case, my minimum acceptable gross margin (60 percent) dictates the amount I can afford to pay for a product. If the numbers don't work I move on.

This ties into the concept that there are two ways to profitability: Sell a lot of product and have a low margin, or have a high margin product and sell a lower volume of product. If you find a product that has a high profit margin and a high volume, you've hit the Holy Grail and you should go and buy an island.

The reality is that most products fit in one category or the other. Naturally the higher the price, the lower the number of units you sell. If you sell expensive diamond necklaces, you probably sell less units per month than say, someone who sells cheap t-shirts. Nevertheless, you can be profitable with either category as long as your margins are solid and your sales volume is high enough.

7. **Lightweight**. If you already have the capacity to ship bulky or heavy products affordably, then congratulations, this point doesn't apply to you. But if not, ask yourself if it might be too expensive to ship your product. Remember, not only do you have to ship it from your manufacturer to

your location; you have to ship to the customer and either you or the customer pays for that expense.

The lighter the product is, the lower your freight costs and the higher your operating margins will be, and also the less likely that your customers will complain about shipping rates. I try to find products that are lightweight and easily packaged. I have my own warehouses, but I would need even more space if all my products were big and heavy.

8. **Unique.** For all of the reasons we've already discussed, you want to sell a unique product. You should also consider complementary products and opportunities for spinoffs or related items that can help you build your product line.

Manufacturer Criteria:

1. **High capacity.** Is your manufacturer really a manufacturer, or are they a trading company? What's their capacity? Many companies have a limited production capacity and can only produce a certain number of units a year. If you start selling 1,000 units a week or a month, can they keep up? It's good to know your manufacturer's capacity *before* you invest a lot of time creating and designing a product with them.

2. **Raw materials.** Supply chain issues are one of the biggest things that ecommerce companies run into as they grow, and the more you can get it mapped out beforehand, the better. What if your manufacturer cannot get aluminum to make your flashlight body or the circuit board they need to make the button switch? You need to unearth those potential pitfalls with your manufacturer in advance and make sure their supply chain is solid.

If you're using this list to evaluate a product you already sell and it doesn't meet all the rules, then try to figure out a way to fix it. Alternatively, continue selling the product until you sell out of inventory, then phase that product out.

Once you've gone through the checklist and made sure your product fits the criteria, let's take a look at two of the ways you can start selling products under your own brand: private label or original products.

Private Label

Private labeling, also known as white labeling, is the easiest way to start selling your own brand of products. It doesn't require engineering, prototyping, and developing a product from the ground up. Instead, private labeling involves finding existing products, potentially modifying them slightly, and branding them with your logo and packaging.

85 to 90 percent of my products are private labeled. You see private label products every time you enter a store or shop online. Kirkland, Great Value, Melissa & Doug, Amazon Basics—those are all big brands and none of them manufacture anything, they're just sticking their label on existing products and selling them as their own.

Private labeling is not the same as selling the same thing everyone else is selling because it builds your brand and bolsters your profits. If the spatula market is booming, for instance, sell a spatula labeled with your brand. You'll make three to five times less selling a Betty Crocker spatula than you would selling your own branded version of the same spatula, which makes a big difference to the profitability of your ecom store.

You can also alter the product–change the color, for example–to better fit your market and differentiate your product from others made by the manufacturer. A lot of people don't bother with modifications; they just stick their label on a product and sell it. That's fine, but taking the extra time and effort to customize the product can help your product stand out. I suggest you build out the basics of your brand by creating a naming structure, logo and a packaging concept first, and then take that to the manufacturer when you start private labeling one of the products they produce. You may think you need to spend tens of thousands of dollars to make your first order, but the truth is that many of the manufacturers already have their product in stock and are willing to let you place orders with quantities as low as a few hundred units. You can still leverage economies of scale even if your quantities are low because you are interacting with manufacturers who are already producing the item. All they have to do is slap a new logo on the product and put it in a box for you.

Alibaba is the most popular platform for sourcing private-label products from China and other foreign countries. Manufacturers all over the world find clients and make money through Alibaba. These manufacturers always have a Minimum Order Quantity (MOQ), but it's not bad. You may have to buy 500 or 1,000 units per order, but you won't have to buy 50,000 units. Be aware that just because a company is listed on Alibaba that does not make them legitimate nor does it mean that they are a manufacturer. Many of the companies on there are trading companies which are in effect middlemen who buy from manufacturers, mark the products up, and then sell them through Alibaba or AliExpress.

If you would like to source within the U.S., Google is your best friend. But I want to warn you that if you're looking for a U.S. source, you may have to go deep in the search results to find them. Most U.S. manufacturers have terrible websites that don't appear on the first or even second page of search results.

Original Equipment Manufacturing (OEM)

Private labeling is one way of building a brand, but it doesn't always fit your needs. If you have an idea for a new product that is not on the market, or if the modifications you want to make to a private-label product change it significantly, consider original equipment manufacturing (OEM).

OEM involves working with the factory from the ground up to create a prototype of an original product. It's a much more involved process than private labeling, but if you have a product idea and you have done the research that shows your customers want it, it can be worth the effort. However, if you are starting your first ecom business, don't put the cart before the horse! Try private labeling first, and once you establish your brand and have the finances to support an OEM project, go for it.

I've created my own products and now they are some of my best sellers, but I did not jump into OEM immediately. I built my businesses first, and while in business, I realized that there was a specific kind of tactical flashlight that the market wanted but that didn't exist. I looked up all the manufacturers I could find who made flashlights, and there are a lot of them, but no one made the type of tactical flashlight I was looking for.

When I found this hole in the market, I approached a manufacturer, showed them a spec sheet, and I asked them if they could make the flashlight. We went back and forth, revised the design, and hired someone to create a couple CAD (computer aided drafting) designs.

I sunk about $35,000 in that project to get the first 1,000 flashlights produced. There were many one-time fees, like mold fees, plate charges, packaging fees, and back and forth shipping charges for the various prototypes, that had to be paid upfront before a sellable unit could even be produced. While the initial 1,000-unit minimum order was expensive, the next 1,000 units (and all orders thereafter) were cheaper because I had already paid those one-time costs.

I wound up with a completely custom flashlight that sells for $89.95 with a per-unit cost of less than $18. However, I wouldn't have done this when I was starting out. I could only do it because I was running a successful business, where I knew what my customers wanted and had the cash flow to invest in such a project.

If you already have a successful ecommerce business, don't shy away from OEM. With 3D printing and other technological advances in rapid prototyping, the cost of manufacturing a product from scratch is just a *fraction* of what it was even five years ago. At least find out how much it'll cost, because a quote is free.

I learned this lesson the hard way, because I once almost missed a great OEM opportunity. I used to own a pet lover's ecom store that sold pendants shaped like animals and custom mugs with pictures of pets. Some of my best-selling products featured Siberian huskies. Many of my customers loved the idea of a Siberian husky pendant; they constantly posted on my company Facebook page asking for one.

I wanted to satisfy my customers (and make more money), so I found a graphic designer to create a 3D CAD drawing of a Siberian husky shaped pendant. I initially decided to make the pendants out of sterling silver, but later found out it was too expensive. The final product would've had to sell for at least $100, which I knew was outside my customers' comfort zone, so I decided to go with a rhodium-plated design instead.

After some research I found a jewelry manufacturer on Alibaba that worked with JCPenney and Sears, so I was confident they produced quality products. I sent them my Siberian husky illustrations with a specs sheet detailing the size, chain length, and packaging for rhodium-plated pendants. They agreed to do it, but they told me that they needed to make a mold first and I would have to pay for it.

That stopped me in my tracks. The only experience I ever had with anything related to a mold was a story from one of my father's friends who was in the injection molding business, who had to make a mold that cost him $100,000 just for the prototype.

When the jewelry manufacturer said the word 'mold' I thought, "Oh crap! This is going to cost me a ton of money." I immediately stopped everything and gave up on the pendant idea without even asking the manufacturer how much it would actually cost.

Four months later, I was on stage at an event talking about product sourcing and manufacturing. I brought up this story and someone asked me, "How much did the mold actually cost?" I realized I actually didn't know. I was so scared of the cost that I never got back to the manufacturer, even though a quote is completely free!

I decided to send the manufacturer an email apologizing and asking how much the mold would cost. Guess what? It was only $150, and that was a one-time cost.

I ordered 2,000 pendants to start, and my actual unit cost for each pendant was around 60¢. By the time I shipped them into the U.S. they were about $1, and I sold every single one for $24.95. I could fit 2,000 of them into a little two-foot by two-foot box, so they were amazing for storage and shipping too.

I almost never made that successful product because I was too nervous about the price of OEM. The moral of the story is that the cost of OEM is not as terrifying as you may think. If you ask for a quote and it falls outside your means at the moment, that is fine; at least you'll have an idea of the expense. Shelve your product idea, create a private label product in the same niche, and use that to build your brand and create a customer base until you are ready to make a product of your own.

Is Your Product Viable?

I once coached someone who wanted me to help him grow his business in exchange for equity. He had developed a set of unique pistol sights that had some quasi-science backing it up, and he thought his product was great. He took out a lot of loans to research, build prototypes, and get the pistol sights into production.

Unfortunately, even though the quality was high, the product itself was mediocre at best. It was basically a novelty, and he expected people who were passionate about guns to adopt it. Unsurprisingly the market didn't like it, especially for the price he wanted to sell it for.

A lower-end market would have been interested in buying his product as a novelty, but this guy's prices drove those customers away. He went into debt bringing his product to life. If he had looked at his product critically at the beginning, he would have NEVER gotten into manufacturing. From the ground up, it was just a bad idea.

Don't be that guy. You should know ALL the numbers before you get into production. There's a lot of educated guesswork that goes into it, but the more educated you are, the less likely you'll be to end up with a failure.

Outside the Box

It's a rule of thumb that your customers will always consume more than you could ever put in front of them. By nature, we as humans are consumers and we live in a world driven by consumption, don't make the mistake of thinking that your customers are ever 'done' buying. If they've purchased everything you offer that appeals to them, they will not spend any additional money with you unless you have something *more* or *different* to offer. If they're not buying it from you, they are buying it from someone else.

Luckily, there are some innovative ways to satisfy these customers and increase your revenue without requiring a significant capital investment. Print on demand, crowdsourcing, crowdfunding, and digital products can all pad your income and give your customers something new to purchase.

Print On Demand

The new print on demand (POD) companies that have materialized in the last five years are one of the biggest (and easiest) ways to increase your company's revenue stream. POD technology involves selling custom merchandise that is printed and created *only when an order is placed*.

When an order comes in, the POD company immediately produces the product and ships it within a few days (sometimes even 24 hours). There's no inventory sitting in a warehouse costing you money, and these platforms usually have no out-of-pocket costs. You just create your design and promote it to your customers via email, on social media, through an ad, or by some other means. You then make money every time someone buys.

A good example of a POD company is CreateSpace, which is owned by (guess who) Amazon. CreateSpace makes print-on-demand books, CDs, and DVDs. You can have a book that's not in any physical inventory for sale on your website, and when a customer places an order, CreateSpace prints the book, binds it, packages it, and ships it within two days straight to the customer.

Amazon.com also offers Amazon Merch, which makes POD t-shirts and apparel. You could create your own custom t-shirt design, make a mock-up, and put it up on your store. If customers buy it, Amazon Merch prints the shirt, packages it, and ships it to the customer. Amazon Merch charges a fee for the service, then you set the price the product sells for and your profit is the difference.

My good friend Don Wilson owns another POD company called GearBubble that provides a similar service. GearBubble makes shirts, mugs, necklaces, bracelets, and all kinds of different promotional and general merchandise. You can create an entire store on his platform, or you can incorporate the products into your store. Simply hire a graphic designer to create designs for mugs, t-shirts, and whatever else you want, and add them to your store–GearBubble handles the printing, packaging, and fulfillment. There's no inventory to worry about, and they even handle customer service.

Crowdfunding

Crowdfunding collects funds from people all over the world to bring a product to the market. It's ideal for making sure there's interest before you start production, or if you don't have the funding to produce a product on your own.

Crowdfunding websites can also create massive viral traction and excitement for your business. If you have a great product idea and you are willing to create a good campaign, crowdfunding can be an excellent way to launch your product and get viral exposure.

To set up a crowdfunding campaign, use a platform like Kickstarter or Indiegogo. Once you create a campaign detailing what you want to produce, anyone can donate and become an investor. They do not get equity, but they do get a guarantee that you'll ship them your product once it has been made, along with any other bonuses or perks you offer to those who help fund the campaign.

Crowdsourcing

Crowdsourcing is a combination of print-on-demand and crowdfunding, and is most commonly seen utilized in the apparel markets.

Before crowdsourcing, you had to go to screen printer with a design and the funds to buy a set number of shirts. You also had to buy enough of every size you wanted to sell. The problem is that you never know what sizes will sell well, and often you end up with a lot of extra inventory that does not sell, and takes up a lot of space.

Crowdsourcing eliminates those problems completely, and it's also cheaper than print-on-demand, because these platforms can pass on the large volume savings to you, which means that the more units you sell the lower the cost of each unit. The average profit on a crowdsourcing platform is $10 to $15. You can sell hoodies, tank tops, anything really. It's a great outside-the-box strategy because it literally has no upfront cost, and apparel has a high perceived value to consumers.

Here's how it works on Teespring, one of the most popular crowdsourcing platforms. You design a shirt in several styles (t-shirts, long sleeves, hoodies, etc.), and then create a campaign that lasts for a set amount of time, like 10 days. The company gives you a link to promote your design in your store, email newsletter, or social media accounts. You set a minimum on the number of shirts you'll produce for the campaign based on the profit margin you want; if you don't mind a low profit margin, you can set the cap as low as 10 shirts, but if you want a high profit margin, you can cap the campaign at 100 shirts.

Everyone who buys the shirt is added to a pre-order list, and once the number of preorders reaches your cap, the campaign 'tips', the customers are charged, and you can continue selling shirts until the campaign ends. Then Teespring starts printing your design and shipping the t-shirt. If you do not reach your minimum tipping point in the time limit you set, the campaign fails and your pre-order customers card does not get charged.

Crowdsourcing sites launched a huge craze of t-shirt sellers that sell hundreds of thousands of shirts every month. One of my Black Label Mastermind members, Matt Stafford, owns Canvus, one of the best apparel crowdsourcing platforms. He combines crowdsourcing with metrics tracking, data analytics, and everything else marketers need to track their sales. You can plug it right into your ecommerce platform, run ads on it, and see the conversion of your ads. Teespring gives you time-based campaigns that expire, while Canvus offers those as well, along with evergreen campaigns that start over every time you hit your target.

Don't Forget About Digital Products

We are ecommerce retailers and we sell physical products. It's only natural for us to get tunnel vision and focus only on physical products and forget the potential of digital products, but that's a big mistake.

So few ecommerce retailers spend any time or effort on digital products, which is a real shame, because digital products can dramatically increase your profits, as well as differentiate you from the competition. If you can mix digital products in with your physical products to create unique product bundles that increase the price of an order or to sell as an upsell for additional profit maximization, you'll make a LOT more money.

In Chapter 2, you learned about digital memberships, newsletters, and other forms of continuity. Many of the same advantages apply to digital products in general. Digital products have virtually no distribution costs; they sell well, especially when combined with physical products as a bundle or an upsell; they can be used to increase the perceived value of your physical product while at the same time letting you charge a few extra dollars; they can be upsold as separate products or as a continuity. Basically, they're simple to create, deliver, have amazing profit margins, and you are nuts not to be leveraging them inside your business.

Every ecommerce business can benefit from implementing digital products, even on a small scale. Digital products don't have to be your best sellers, but any time they sell, they practically have a 100 percent profit margin that goes straight to your operating capital. Every little sale is a big boost to your operating profit margin because there are little to no COGS or other costs associated with it.

Even if only one percent of your customers buy your digital offerings, it adds up. Those earnings could easily cover your car payment, or even your mortgage payment, each month.

There's a skincare company owned by a Black Label Mastermind member that does an excellent job including digital products into their business. They have $37 anti-aging skin care guide that shows up as an order bump when customers add an anti-aging cream or serum in their cart and go to the checkout page. Over 20 percent of the company's customers take this $37 order bump. It's $37 of PURE PROFIT from a digital product offered by an ecommerce business that sells physical products.

If you sell a product that everybody else is selling—and this is huge on Amazon—offering a digital accompaniment gives you a way of standing out, as well as increasing profits. Let say you're selling sports tape along with dozens of other companies. Instead of just selling the tape, you include a PDF guide with the 12 best tape wrapping methods to prevent injuries. You can now sell the tape for $3 or $4 more a roll because you're providing more value. That extra price increase is pure profit.

Digital products are so easy to create–you can make videos, PDFs, a piece of software, a calculator, or even a spreadsheet. Anything that provides increased value to your customer is fair game. But remember, digital products work best in more tightly focused niches. The more specific the type of products you sell on your store, the better your conversion rates for digital products will be.

Product Fulfillment

In ecommerce, you don't have a retail store where customers can immediately get their products. Instead, your customers are buying online. They could be anywhere in the world, and you have to somehow get your products to them after they purchase.

There are four main product fulfillment methods for online businesses that you can use to get your products to your customers: Arbitrage, drop shipping, third-party fulfillment, and in-house fulfillment. Read on to find out which one is right for your business.

Arbitrage

Arbitrage has become popular in the last few years because it requires very little effort or upfront expense. All you have to do is find a good product that is already on sale on AliExpress, eBay, or another online shopping site, and then list the product in your ecom store with a price that is higher than the other place is selling it for. When the product sells, return to

AliExpress or eBay, buy it, and have it shipped directly to the customer. You make your money on the difference between your higher sale price and the price you buy it for. Most arbitrage like this happens through AliExpress, Alibaba's little brother. AliExpress allows manufacturers and trading companies to sell products in retail quantities, so you can buy one or two of the item instead of 500 units or more.

Unfortunately, there are a lot of big issues with arbitrage. First, you are NOT in control of the product. What if the platform you use only has four items left and you just sold 20 of them? Second, the product usually ships from China, and while they usually ship for free, there's often a three to five-week waiting period (assuming they bother to ship quickly) before the product reaches your customer. That's a long time to wait, and customers don't like that.

Also, retail products shipped from China are usually sent to the U.S. via ePacket shipping (China's value shipping option). Most shippers use this method to get around paying import and export duties, and U.S. Customs Service is starting to crack down on it. Payment processors and merchant account providers like PayPal *hate* businesses that use international arbitrage because of the high charge-back rates from unhappy customers. Many arbitrage vendors get shut down right after Christmas because they sell thousands of products to customers who don't receive them until February.

The arbitrage model is less problematic when you use a domestic retail platform like eBay, but that comes with its own complications. eBay typically involves someone packing the product at home and shipping it to the customer. It's not scalable and there's a lot more risk involved, but it's still compelling to many sellers because it doesn't require any upfront capital investment.

I've tried arbitrage and despite its many shortcomings, I think it's good for one thing: testing products. Let's say you want a new private label item for your store. First you can find a similar item on a platform like AliExpress, put your marketing message together, and try to sell it. Use arbitrage as a test to see if the product has the potential before approaching a manufacturer.

Under all other circumstances, I recommend avoiding arbitrage because you're basically playing with fire. You can't build your brand on this model, and you'll be lucky to even keep your business open after your customers start demanding refunds due to delayed shipping.

There's also no telling whether the U.S. Customs Service will go after your sellers and charge them for duties and taxes owed. Customs is known for checking imports as far back as three years and adding all the unpaid duties into one big fine, and trust me, you don't want to get stuck with that fine.

Drop Ship

Drop shipping has been around forever. It evolved from manufacturers that had lots of extra inventory and decided to make it available to smaller retailers without requiring them to pre-purchase inventory. The manufacturer provides product photos and information, and you list and sell the products in your store. The manufacturer often has an app or some other technology that links your store to their shipping program. When an order comes in, it goes directly to them and ships from their warehouse.

Drop shipping is similar to an arbitrage model, but with a few important differences. These are responsible manufacturers that promptly ship their product, complete with your logo on the receipt or on the shipping label, to the customer. There are many ecom stores that do nothing but drop ship because it lets them offer a whole catalogue of products without having to pay for, or store, any actual inventory.

A lot of people on eBay are also drop shippers; they list a product on eBay and when it sells, the drop shipper ships the product to the customer. They are still technically arbitraging, but it's a much more professional model.

Just like with arbitrage, you can use drop shipping to test a product. When I want to add a product or two to one of my ecom stores, I add the drop ship products first to test the idea. You can also add drop shipping to your business to round out your selection of products.

But while drop shipping is a significant step up from the arbitrage model, it's NOT ideal for a scalable business because it puts you in that 10 to 30 percent gross margin range. You're still selling other people's products like a regular retailer. It's a great way to get started, but your profit margins are terrible, so you should start adding your own products as soon as you can.

Third-Party Fulfillment

Third-party fulfillment involves buying inventory and finding a fulfillment house to store, pick, pack, and ship your products to your customers as they sell. Think of a fulfillment house as the shipping department of your company. Every time a customer places an order in your ecom store, their shipping and order details automatically go to the fulfillment house for processing.

Fulfillment houses take care of branding as well: you can send special packaging to the fulfillment house, and the they can put your brand name on the shipping label and packing slip. Most fulfillment houses charge a fee per order or item sold to cover shipping costs, with an additional monthly fee for storage if your inventory does not turn over quickly enough.

Third-party fulfillment is useful in many situations. They are great for business owners who don't want to deal with the hassle of packaging and shipping their products to customers. With a fulfillment house, these business owners can be in ecommerce without ever touching shipping supplies.

Fulfillment houses are also enticing because they typically ship large volumes of packages every day, and because the shipping companies give them significant discounts on their shipping rates, these discounts usually get passed on to you as well. These discounts are often much bigger than you could get on your own. I use a fulfillment house for one of my companies, and I'm currently getting a 45 percent discount off list rate when they ship through FedEx.

Fulfillment houses can be useful even if you fulfill products in-house. Let's say a company is on the West Coast and gets a lot of East Coast orders. They notice some customer dissatisfaction with the shipping time from West Coast to East Coast, so they hire a third-party fulfillment company based on the East Coast and store half their inventory there.

Once this company has a 3rd party east coast fulfillment house in place, they set up their shipping software to automatically send East Coast orders there. This company is essentially using the fulfillment house as their East Coast distribution center without having to actually build one. In a similar vein, third-party fulfillment is also a good solution for international merchants who live abroad but have customers in the U.S. They can't ship efficiently from Sweden or Russia or wherever they are, so they use a third-party fulfillment house in the U.S. to fulfill and ship their products.

A good example of third-party fulfillment is Amazon FBA. You may remember that Amazon FBA lets you ship your products to Amazon in advance. Amazon stores, packs, and ships the products to your customers. It even has automatic integration with Shopify and other major ecommerce platforms; if someone buys your product from your Shopify store and you use Amazon FBA, Amazon will take one of your products out of inventory and ship it to your customer even though it wasn't purchased on Amazon.

The downside of Amazon FBA is the packaging. They put everything in an Amazon box with their branded tape, so it looks like your product came directly from Amazon (which it did). This is not ideal if you want to build your brand, and Amazon's fulfillment fees are typically higher than you would find in a normal 3rd party fulfillment service.

In-House Fulfillment

In-house fulfillment is exactly what it sounds like–you either have a warehouse or a garage at your business that you use to print, pack, and ship your own products. If you have a large inventory, you'll need a warehouse and your overhead costs will go up. A lot of companies start in their garage and then scale as they grow; other companies use third-party fulfillment from the beginning.

The downside of this option, in addition to the extra cost, is that you become a fulfillment business in addition to an ecom business. It's a lot more involved. You have to deal with shipping services like UPS and FedEx, custom packaging, warehouse staff, inventory systems, tracking, theft, loss—all the logistics that a third-party fulfillment company would do on your behalf. In exchange for that, you get *complete control* over your order process and the customer experience, and sometimes that is worth the hassle.

I started with third-party fulfillment, but I grew at such a fast rate that fulfillment companies had trouble keeping up. As my business evolved I wanted to do a lot of customizations on my shipments, but my ideas were too complicated for the third-party fulfillment companies.

I also had a bad experience with a fulfillment house in Idaho that failed to ship my products for several months. I had a lot of dissatisfied and angry customers, and my merchant account was closed because of my high charge-back rates. It could have destroyed my reputation and business, and it took a lot to recover.

Because of that fiasco and my desire to use more customized shipping processes, I decided to bring my product fulfillment in-house. Now, I control the entire fulfillment process. I can monitor the entire customer experience, create my own marketing methods, and come up with a more branded message. I can also test offers on the fly by including them in the packages we ship out.

Basically, it's easier for me to adapt or make changes, because my fulfillment house is in my office. I don't recommend it for everybody, but it works for me.

There's no reason to feel like you have to start out doing your own fulfillment; it's not a badge of honor, and there's nothing wrong with using a fulfillment house. If your company is growing fast, you may eventually outgrow a third-party fulfillment company, but at that point you should have the revenue and infrastructure to create your own in-house operation.

Conclusion

Knowing your margins, selling the right products, using out-of-the-box extras, and planning out fulfillment are all part of being smart about what you sell. I recommend starting with your margins, since data can change *everything*, and going from there. The little extra products I told you about in the out-of-the-box section can also be easily added to your business.

When getting into making bigger changes, like adding private labeled or OEM products, or creating an in-house fulfillment center, you'll need to make sure you take time to plan out exactly what you are doing, what your needs are for each piece, and that you have the necessary education or training to help you make this a reality. If you want to build a memorable brand with happy customers, you'll eventually need to make these changes.

Chapter 3 Summary

Learn how to calculate the three types of profit margins: gross profit margin, operating profit margin, and net profit margin. Aim for a 150 percent markup on all your products to account for advertising, operational, product, and tax costs.

Always strive to sell your own products and build your brand. Start with private labeling until you have the revenue for OEM.

Your customers always consume more than you can ever put in front of them, so be ready to try outside-the-box methods like print-on-demand, crowdfunding, and digital products.

There are four main product fulfillment methods that are suitable for online businesses: arbitrage, drop ship, third-party fulfillment, and in-house fulfillment. I recommend the first two for testing products and the latter two for shipping your existing products.

CHAPTER 4

CONVERSION TRICKS, SALES BOOSTS, AND PROFIT MAXIMIZERS

It's always easier to work with what you've got than to start something new. So far I've discussed sales funnels, recurring income cores, and products, but I haven't explained how you can make the most of what you have right now.

There are a lot of tricks, boosts, tweaks, and changes you can make to your current business structure to increase its overall effectiveness and growth without having to reinvent the wheel. I use every trick in this section in my own businesses, and I can confidently say I would be at least 30 to 40 percent less profitable if I didn't.

The majority of the students I coach (and that includes you) are missing *70 percent or more* of these tactics in their businesses. If one of my boosts increases your conversion rate by 3 to 5 percent, that can turn into 20 to 90 percent more profit over the lifetime of that customer. In other words, don't skip over this section.

In this chapter, I'll go over a number of different strategies that fall under three main categories: conversion tricks, sales boosts, and profit maximizers. These strategies can have a HUGE effect on your business in the long run, as well as dramatic shifts in the present.

Almost every technique in this chapter is simple to implement, but you also don't have to apply them all at once. Pick one, try it out, reap the benefits, then add another and another until you're using them all.

Conversion Tricks

Conversion tricks are designed to "increase" the number of sales you make from your advertising and marketing efforts. The tricks in this section–retargeting, product reviews, landing pages, and unique mobile checkouts-can all increase your conversions on both the front end and the back end of your business.

Retargeting

Retargeting is a super effective form of advertising that involves tiny snippets of ad-activating code that tracks the actions of your website visitors. When someone visits your page and browses a product without buying it, the code "follows" the person as they visit other web pages and shows them ads for the product. Retargeting pixels also check the web pages the person has *already* visited and displays products or other related offers that may interest them based on that activity.

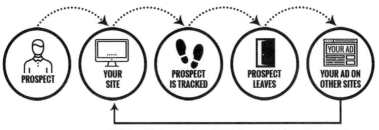

PROSPECT RETURNS TO YOUR SITE

Retargeting doesn't just keep customers thinking about your product; it can make prospects think you're much bigger than you are. Often, they won't realize you're retargeting them at all—they'll simply think you're a massive company that spends lots of money advertising all over the world. It builds awareness, presence, and legitimacy, and that's why people are 70 percent more likely to convert after being retargeted.[15]

Everyone says banner ads (display advertising) are useless because click-through rates can reach as low as 0.07 percent, but retargeted banner ads on average have a 0.7 percent click-through rate (far from useless).[16] And whether you make a sale through retargeting or not, you'll still be at the top of your

[15] Abramovich, G. (2013, November 20). 15 mind-blowing stats about retargeting. Retrieved from http://www.cmo.com/features/articles/2013/11/20/15_Stats_Retargeting.html

[16] Abramovich, G. (2013, November 20). 15 mind-blowing stats about retargeting. Retrieved from http://www.cmo.com/features/articles/2013/11/20/15_Stats_Retargeting.html

prospects' minds. Retargeting garners an impressive 1,046 percent increase in branded search and a 726 percent increase in site visits after just four weeks of continuous retargeting use.[17] [18]

This is a **big deal**. My retargeting campaigns regularly generate over 1,000 percent ROI for my brands. If I really mess up I get 900 percent; if I do well, I get 4,000 percent.

One of my retargeting campaigns cost $11,000 over the lifetime of the campaign, and it brought in almost $241,000. I'd make that trade any day, wouldn't you?

How to Retarget

As far as retargeting services go, I recommend Perfect Audience, AdRoll, and SiteScout in addition to good 'ol Facebook. One of the big mistakes many companies make is to dial in and only use one retargeting service. You should *always* use multiple retargeting networks to run your promotions. Why? Every time you add an additional retargeting network, you reach a significantly larger portion of your audience than you would with only one network.

Some networks also only cover one domain; Facebook, for instance, won't display ads on sites like Google, Bing, and Huffington Post (although soon it'll cover Instagram). Some networks overlap, but your audience still expands every time you add on an additional retargeting network. The same exact

---

[17] Abramovich, G. (2013, November 20). 15 mind-blowing stats about retargeting. Retrieved from
http://www.cmo.com/features/articles/2013/11/20/15_Stats_Retargeting.html

[18] Hayon, A. (2015, March 26). Top 3 ways to improve your retargeting in 2015! Retrieved from https://www.iperceptions.com/blog/top-3-ways-to-improve-your-retargeting-in-2015

ads can run on multiple networks giving you maximum coverage and reach.

At the bare minimum, get coverage on Facebook and one display network. YouTube is another network I highly recommend because it's underutilized. It's cheap and highly effective as a retargeting platform, especially for physical products (video is the next best thing to actually touching a product). You can build retargeting lists on YouTube through the Google AdWords network so that when someone watches a YouTube video, your video ad shows first.

Product Reviews

One of the main reasons Amazon is so popular is because of the customer review system. When people look at a product on Amazon, they immediately scroll down and check out the reviews, sometimes even before looking at the pictures.

That's in contrast with traditional ecom stores, which totally ignore reviews. Many ecommerce stores have a review function, but most of their products have zero reviews.

This is a real shame because product reviews with the right format and rich snippets not only improve trust in your business, but they also boost your search engine rankings. If you visit extremely successful ecommerce stores like Overstock and Target, you'll notice that they emphasize reviews. Overstock in particular is focused on making sure there are tons of customer reviews–they follow up with their customers regularly and ask them to post reviews on the site.

Google loves product reviews, especially reviews with a rich snippet format. Rich snippets let search engines display your reviews right in the search results. That's why when you search for a product, the Amazon link to the product page often displays a star rating under the heading in the Google search results.

Google loves rich snippets because they enhance the Google user experience, and you can easily incorporate rich snippets into your own storefront or pages. My previous system of reviews didn't include rich snippets, but the new system does, and now product pages that never showed up on the search results before pop up on the first and second pages.

You can capitalize on reviews in your store by following just a few simple rules. First, encourage your customers to review your products the same way that Overstock does. When customers buy a product, automatically send them an email asking them to review. Ask them, incentivize them, even send them a little gift with their next order to show them how important their feedback is to your company.

Second, model your reviews after Amazon's reviews. We as consumers are trained to trust the distinctive style, color palate, and five-star look of Amazon reviews. Use that to your advantage by copying that color scheme and five-star rating system. This may seem bizarre, but it works. I changed the default review platform on my Shopify store to mimic the look and feel of Amazon, and we saw a 7 percent global lift in sales from our store. They were the same reviews; I just changed the way they looked.

Display reviews on your product page similar to how they are displayed on Amazon. Many shopping carts have plugins that can configure your review sections to resemble Amazon's. If there's something like that available to you, use it. If not, pay a developer to style your reviews with similar color and layout.

Third, once you've collected reviews and formatted them like Amazon's reviews, don't forget to use rich snippets in your site code to ensure those reviews catch Google's attention. And just like that, your reviews will start boosting sales.

Landing Pages

You may recall landing pages from Chapter 1, since they play an important role in sales funnels. Here I go into more detail on how they work and what they should include.

The landing page, also called a bridge or presell page, is the page customers see before they check out. Landing pages educate your visitors about the benefits of your product and encourage them to hit a "buy" button that bypasses your product listing page and takes them straight to checkout. Most ecommerce business owners have a product listing page generated by their ecommerce platform that could technically be called a landing page, and although it is there to allow customers to buy your product, its format and style is not conducive to increasing their conversion rate.

A real landing page is usually devoid of distractions. You may recall that it's a focused page where visitors get three options: buy your product, bookmark your page, or leave.

The landing page might be the most important tactic in this whole chapter because it guarantees a MASSIVE increase in conversion of traffic into buyers. It's also the tactic most people try to avoid because it takes work. They'd rather slightly tweak their page and eek out marginal gains than spend the time crafting a landing page that can bring in HUGE gains.

Don't make that mistake. Implementing landing pages in my businesses always creates an instant 5 to 10 percent boost for my front-end conversion (much higher than the 1 to 2 percent conversion rate of standard product listing pages). I have some landing pages that have boosted my front end conversion rates as high as 20 percent! In a nutshell, with a landing page you'll spend less on advertising and get more customers and a higher ROI.

Create a landing page for any product you want to send traffic to, especially paid traffic. I use landing pages for all the products I'm promoting, whether I'm doing so through emails, blog posts, or social media ads. The only time my product listing pages are used is when a customer finds them organically.

Components of a Landing Page

All of these components need to be included on your landing page if you want your landing page to work. In my opinion, the video is the only optional component, and I only say it's optional because many people are too scared to make a video featuring their product. If the video is stopping you from getting your page live, just skip it and add it later.

- **Headline.** The headline introduces your product and grabs your prospect's interest.

- **Pictures**. A variety of pictures of the product go below the headline, with the "buy" button on the right. Below that, add more details on the product interspersed with pictures of the product.

- **Video**. All of my best-converting landing pages include a video showcasing the product. It could simply be someone's hands showing the product from various angles, or it could be someone explaining what the product does. If you're selling a product that customers need to learn how to use, you can make your video longer or include multiple short videos that explain each of your product's features. These work exceptionally well, but the videos should be 30 seconds or less unless the product needs a lengthy video for demonstration or educational purposes. Even then, keep the video under three minutes for the best results.

- **Features and benefits.** Every feature should have a matching benefit that explains why the feature is important. If the product is lightweight, for instance, the benefit could be that the customer may be able to carry it in their purse or pocket. List five to ten of these benefits, from most important to least, on the left side of the page (see image below for proper placement).

- **Product reviews.** If your product is already on Amazon, pull your reviews from Amazon. If not, model your reviews after Amazon's reviews. Choose product reviews that praise specific aspects of your product, and put them on the right side of the page so they mirror the features and benefits on the left. Use enough reviews to match the length of the features and benefits (five to seven reviews is generally enough).

- **Purchase incentives.** Offer a discount, a free shipping offer, or a bundle discount. Display these offers prominently wherever you have a "buy" button. Don't incentivize all the time, or your customers will become blind to your incentives and they'll lose their effectiveness.

- **Retargeting pixels.** Retargeting has a dramatic impact on sales, and your landing page is the first crucial chance to snag sales. Drop pixels (retargeting code snippets) from multiple retargeting platforms on your landing page so that when someone visits the page, but does not buy, they are automatically retargeted with ads designed to bring them back to purchase. If they do buy, a different set of retargeting ads will be shown that can offer them a different, but complementary product you sell.

- **Exit-intent email grab.** This is a window that pops up when a visitor tries to leave your page without buying. At that point you've already lost the potential sale as they have decided to leave without making a purchase, but if you get their email address, you can follow up with them and potentially get them to purchase at a later time. Remember NO means *"not now"*, NOT *"not ever"*. The email grab offers a lead magnet, more content, a discount, or another incentive in exchange for the visitor's email address Only a small percentage of your traffic will take this offer, but it's still enough to make a sizable boost in your income.

* Retargeting pixel goes in code

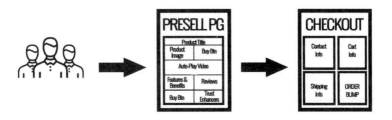

Unique Mobile Checkout

I already touched on the power of mobile business in Principle 9. Just to remind you how powerful it really is, I want to share this statistic with you: in 2015, mobile users accounted for 29.7 percent of all ecommerce sales,[19] and this number is supposed to DOUBLE soon.

Here's another tidbit that may interest you–44 percent of the traffic to my Second Amendment business is from mobile, and that number is constantly growing. This is something you need to make sure you are capitalizing on correctly and *fast*.

The major downside of mobile ecommerce for the user is that many online checkout processes are unfriendly toward mobile users. One of the best ways to take advantage of all the mobile traffic is to create a unique and user friendly checkout process for mobile and tablet users. I'm referring to a completely separate checkout process that is only activated when a user is on mobile or on a tablet, and does not show when a user is on a regular computer. When the shopping cart recognizes a mobile user, it bypasses the standard web checkout and activates the mobile-friendly checkout. Add a mobile checkout app to your store yourself, or hire a developer to customize it for you.

---

[19] Brohan, M. (2015, August 18). Mobile commerce is now 30% of all U.S. e-commerce. Retrieved from https://www.internetretailer.com/2015/08/18/mobile-commerce-now-30-all-us-e-commerce

What are the components of a unique mobile checkout process? First, it's much simpler. All the extra images or styling elements you normally have on your checkout page may not scale down correctly on a mobile device and should be removed. Any fancy code that may trigger popups or on-the-fly calculations also don't translate well on mobile and should be eliminated.

Second, mobile checkouts typically have more than one page because on mobile devices, it's hard to enter a ton of data on a single page. It's much easier to enter smaller amounts of data on two or three smaller pages. Smaller screens naturally work better with smaller chunks of data, so a multi-step checkout process is ideal on a mobile device.

Third, don't force the customer to create an account in order to check out! This step causes a 23 percent average abandonment rate for shopping carts.[20] You can still ask customers to create an account, but do it after their payment has been completed so as not to interfere with checkout.

Finally, add a prominent PayPal checkout option. PayPal is one of the best and most mobile-friendly checkout options available. Credit card payments are a pain on mobile devices, and many people are wary of entering their credit card information on a mobile device. Adding PayPal as a mobile checkout option produced a 12 percent boost in our checkout process on mobile.

Sales Boosts

Sales boosts are exactly what they sound like–tricks that catch customers and incentivize them to buy both now and in

---

[20] Patel, N. (n.d.). 5 ecommerce stats that will make you change your entire marketing approach. Retrieved from https://blog.kissmetrics.com/5-ecommerce-stats/

the future. You already learned about order bumps, one of the most effective sales boosts in Chapter 1. Loss leaders, trip wires, flash sales, and phone calls also increase sales, and together they make a powerful and lucrative revenue stream for your business.

Loss Leaders

A loss leader is a product that is sold below product or fulfillment cost. They are called "loss leaders" because you actually *lose* money on these sales. For example, if a product costs $10 and you sell it for $5, it's a loss leader.

Since you lose money on these deals, you should only use them to acquire new customers, not to stir up repeat business. Loss leaders are a great way to get new customers in the door, but they should only be used if you have a sales funnel in place to recoup the loss right away so that you can at least break even, if not turn a small profit.

Say your local grocery store has a special discount on a product you love. When you go to get the item, you're likely to buy other things too. The store is willing to lose a little bit of money on a particular product (their loss leader) to get you into the store where, more often than not, you wind up buying more items.

One of the best examples of loss leader marketing is the free plus shipping offer (the customer gets a free item and only pays for shipping). I use free plus shipping offers every day in all of my businesses, and I spend upwards of 30 percent of my marketing budget on driving traffic to them. The free product often only costs the business a few dollars, and we have a high-converting sales funnel with high-converting products behind it that leaves us with a nice profit even after absorbing the loss leader costs.

While this strategy pays off, I couldn't have done it when I first started. I had to learn the metrics of my business and my sales funnels so that I could structure everything to be profitable, despite starting out with a loss. This is just one more piece of evidence that the more money and the more data you have, the more you can afford to spend to catch the customer (see Principle 10).

Tripwires

Tripwires are low-cost offers designed to get people to try out your company. Like loss leaders, they are meant to increase your customer base by giving prospective customers a way to try out your company for a low price. Tripwires should be positioned as the front end product of a connected sales funnel that features related upsells designed to sell the customer additional products.

Unlike loss leaders, tripwires don't result in a loss; businesses usually make a small profit or break even on them. Because they don't lose money, it's okay to use tripwires on existing customers. Tripwires are also great for reactivating customers who haven't purchased in a long time.

Tripwire pricing depends on the pricing threshold of the market. If a business' products are all $100 or more, then a tripwire can be a $60 or $70 item; if everything is priced around $30, then a tripwire is a $10 or $7 item.

Whatever the cost, though, your business should NOT be made up of tripwires. Multiple tripwires are okay, but if you wind up with a business full of tripwires and no more profitable items, you'll have no way to make bigger profits. Tripwires are just a tool for getting more customers into your sales funnels.

Flash Sales

Flash sales are 24-hour events that you can send to both your customers and prospects (the people who have joined your list but haven't bought your products yet). Flash sales can include a steep discount on a product, a big sale, or a bundle of products for a discounted price, but they should still result in a profit on each sale.

Some companies even include a timer on their website during flash sales that counts down until the sale expires–it whips customers into a frenzy. Groupon and other coupon sites do this all the time.

Flash sales can be done on the fly, but they can be planned out in advance for greater effect. If you know you have a slow sales period approaching, you can schedule a flash sale and send out an email promotion alerting your customers. This tactic will create a sales spike during that normally slow period.

The Phone Doesn't Bite

I firmly believe that every ecommerce business should have a phone number that customers can call to reach a real person. This personal touch is lost in many ecommerce businesses, but it works wonders. It's a sales boost, a conversion trick, and a customer satisfaction enhancer.

The first benefit of adding a phone number is sales. I've found that as soon as I made a phone number available to my customers, I had an almost *30 percent boost* in daily orders. Some callers have difficulty with your website, and providing another option allows these customers to still place their order. Also many potential customers do not feel comfortable providing their credit card online, but will happily provide those same details over the phone.

Second, having calling capabilities can help salvage declined orders. Most sales platforms offer a setting that automatically sends declined orders to accounts receivable. If you have a phone line, someone can call the customer quickly (preferably within ten minutes) and say, "I noticed you tried to order and it didn't go through. Can I help you fix this?"

A single hire dedicated to doing this can produce exponential profits in your company, reducing declined orders by 80 percent, in my experience. If you empower your sales team to sell other products as well, you can generate additional profit for your business.

Having a phone service is also great for customer loyalty. I can't tell you how many customers called in to either make an order or report an issue, only to then post on our Facebook page or product listings to praise my store's customer service after the call. This is free advertising that may influence other people to shop at your store.

A good friend of mine in software sales, Joe Troyer, is so sold on this idea that he only allows phone support. He doesn't have any email support at all, and his customer service team generates enough in sales profits to cover his entire overhead. I'm not saying you shouldn't have email support, but you should have at least one phone operator to handle all of your declined orders as soon as they happen, as well as to take phone orders.

Profit Maximizers

Profit Maximizers are designed to increase your business' overall profits in as many areas as possible. You may not have considered using free shipping to increase average order size, leveraging shipping and handling as a profit center, or getting paid to include ride-alongs in your packaging, but all this and more can make your customers happy and strengthen your bottom line.

Free Shipping

Everybody loves free shipping, and when used strategically, it can be a huge benefit to your business. Unfortunately, free shipping is often misused in the ecommerce space, especially by small companies that feel obligated to offer it. My rule is that free shipping should always be used strategically, NOT as a desperate grab for more sales.

The best way to use free shipping is as an incentive to increase your store's average order value. This strategy is by far the most common trick used by big e-tailers to boost their AOV; think about how many popular online stores have a special offer for free shipping on orders over a certain dollar amount. This tactic is popular for a reason; 58 percent of customers are willing to buy more items if they then qualify for free shipping.[21]

Every ecommerce business has an average cart size or checkout value. To really benefit from free shipping, you should only offer free shipping on orders that are LARGER than your average order size. If your average cart size is $20, offer customers free shipping on orders over $35. This

---

[21] Dreyer, K. (2014, June 11). Study: Consumers demand more flexibility when shopping online. Retrieved from https://www.comscore.com/Insights/Press-Releases/2014/6/Study-Consumers-Demand-More-Flexibility-When-Shopping-Online

encourages your customers to add another item or two to their order so they qualify for free shipping and it works like crazy.

In my businesses, I only offer free shipping when a customer's cart is 20 percent over my average order value. The effectiveness of this tactic depends on your store, product, and average order value; with my "over 20 percent" threshold, I usually see a 30 to 50 percent boost in sales.

Why do people spend so much more when they get free shipping? Well, if a free shipping discount activates when a customer buys 20 percent more than your average order value, people won't stop at 20 percent—usually they spend *more*.

The likelihood of a customer finding a product on your store that adds exactly 20 percent to their initial cart value is low. So not only can you get 58 percent more customers to buy with a free shipping incentive, but you can also get that 58 percent to spend at least 20 percent *more* per order. Just don't forget to frequently remind your customers (as they shop) that they can get free shipping if they spend that target amount.

Another strategy employed by sites like Bodybuilding.com is displaying exactly how much more the customer has to spend to get free shipping. Once they reach the checkout page, the site says, "If you spend 'x' more dollars, you qualify for free shipping." The best place for this type of offer is right where the shipping charges are listed.

Telling the customer how much more they have to spend to get free shipping is a great way to increase your average order size without randomly giving out free shipping. Alternatively, you can offer the customer free shipping if they add just *one* more item. It's a last-ditch effort that's easy to code on most shopping carts.

Note that if you follow the advice in this book, your average order size will naturally increase. Make sure to increase the threshold your customers have to hit to qualify for free shipping as well. You don't want that amount to remain stagnant as your average order value rises.

Shipping and Handling as a Profit Center

Many ecommerce business owners believe that they have to *lose* money on shipping in order to be competitive. This is not true, but making money from shipping only works when you're moving lots of volume yourself or a third-party fulfillment center is willing to pass the shipping discount onto you. If you're not there yet, file this profit maximizer away for later.

I pass my shipping discounts on to my customers, but I also add a dollar to the shipping charge *before* presenting it to the customer. Some companies use a percentage, but I like a $1 bump (a percentage may inflate the shipping price too much, and I like to give my customers a good deal).

My t-shirt business adds $1 to the shipping charge for every package that goes out the door. With our discounted rates, the domestic shipping cost for a t-shirt is roughly $3.50, so I charge my customers $4.50. If I didn't have a discount from the shipping company, my shipping rate would probably be $6 or $8 to ship that same shirt; at that point, it wouldn't be feasible to add anything to the shipping cost because it would already be too expensive for many customers.

Because my volume is so high, I can discount shipping and pass it on to the customer, but I still make a $1 profit on every order shipped. Last week, for example, I shipped out over 1,400 orders through my Oregon facility. That means I earned an extra $1,400 in profit just from shipping.

Ride-Alongs

If you've ever ordered products in the mail, you may have noticed little paper advertisements included in the package. Those are ride-alongs–printed inserts or flyers included in a package when it ships. They're a great, inexpensive way to make extra sales, test out new offers, and even make extra cash from third-party advertisers.

You can easily include ride-alongs in packages yourself if you have in-house fulfillment, or some 3rd party fulfillment houses will do it for a small fee. Note that if you're on Amazon, you can't use inserts unless you include the ride-alongs inside the actual product packaging; Amazon won't include inserts in their boxes.

One great thing about package inserts is that they are cheap. My most expensive insert costs less than 3¢ because I buy it in bulk. One sale pays for all the inserts, and after two sales, I make a profit. It's a negligible cost with a big upside.

Inserts can also be highly targeted. If a customer buys product A, you can send them Insert A. If they buy product B, you can send them insert B. The cost of delivering this message has already been paid for because the customer has paid for shipping.

There are many kinds of inserts: discount coupons, liquidation offers, even product samples. They're a great way to move unpopular products–just make a special discount offer for 70 percent off to get the product moving.

You can also use ride-alongs to promote your brand. You could include a card asking your customer to post a product review after they've tried the product. You can also include a nice 'thank you' card to let your customers know you value them and their patronage.

Inserts can increase loyalty and make customers feel special. With my Second Amendment brand, for every new customer that places an order, I include a 50 percent discount coupon for their next order in our stores. It's a one-time incentive that I offer to all my new customers, since they come from funnels and have never been to my store. I have a 30 to 40 percent take rate on that coupon within two weeks of when the first order was placed.

I not only make a small profit, but I also train the customer to go to my store, where they can browse and perhaps make a second purchase. The chances of getting this same customer to purchase a third time are then significantly higher.

Another benefit to using inserts is that when your customer base is large enough, other companies actually *pay* you to include their insert in your package. You also have the option of becoming an affiliate for a product that your company doesn't supply. You can create your own flyer to send out to your customers, and if customers buy using the link on your insert, you get paid a commission. I do this all the time—I find a complimentary product that I feel good about supporting and sharing with my customers, and if my customers buy the product through the link in the insert, I get paid. It's basically free money.

Conclusion

All of the little conversion tricks, sales boosts, and profit maximizers in this chapter add up to BIG changes in the overall profits of your company. Changing one thing may create only a one percent increase in your business, but if you make five of those changes, you've made a 5 percent change on the front end that incrementally compounds in the back end. Like I said before, a 5 percent increase in customer retention alone can equal almost a 95 percent boost in long-term profits.

Not sure where to start? Work on the easier boosts and build up to the more difficult ones. Retargeting, product reviews, ride-alongs, order bumps, and free shipping offers are all easy to implement. If you're shipping large volumes, you can also try to make a profit on your shipping. Start there, build on it, and your profits will start increasing by leaps and bounds.

Chapter 4 Summary

Conversion tricks (retargeting, product reviews, landing pages, and unique mobile checkout) help you turn more of your website visitors into customers. Retargeting advertises to website visitors who don't buy; product reviews create trust; landing pages increase conversions; and unique mobile checkout makes it easier for mobile users to purchase. You should use all of them to get the most customers.

Sales boosts (loss leaders, tripwires, flash sales, and a phone number) lure buyers in with unbeatable deals. Loss leaders cost you money and should only be used for customer acquisition; tripwires break even or make a little money and can be used on anyone, including existing customers; flash sales turn a profit, still provide a discount and can also be used on anyone. All of these should lead customers into sales funnels to improve order value.

Profit maximizers (free shipping, shipping and handling as a profit center, and ride-alongs) increase profit from existing customers. Free shipping can inflate order value; shipping and handling discounts can make you extra profit on each order; and ride-alongs create more sales from your customers while offering the potential for affiliate commissions.

PART II

● ●

EVOLVED
INTELLIGENCE

It's no surprise that research and intelligence gathering is the most neglected aspect of an ecommerce business. Research is not attractive; it's actually the least attractive part of business because the only way to do it is with the application of lots of time and effort.

But you have to understand this: one of the best ways an ecommerce business can grow exponentially is through evolved intelligence–gaining a deeper understanding of its market. Evolved intelligence is about knowing your customers, your competition, and the magic of big data, and it can change everything. It may not be exciting or fun, but the reality is that the more current your intelligence, the better your company's ability to produce a profit, adapt to changes in the market, and dominate your competition.

Pioneer marketer and advertising guru John Wanamaker once said this:

"Half the money I spend on advertising is wasted; the trouble is I don't know which half."[22]

This accurately captures the problems of marketing. You'll always have waste in your marketing budget, especially when it comes to advertising and promotion, but with evolved intelligence you can dramatically cut down that waste and redistribute it to things that give you a good ROI.

Much of the research and work in Part II is labor intensive. You can give the more basic parts to a project manager or an assistant to work through, but I recommend that you do some of the work yourself. It can be partially outsourced or

---

[22] Chait, G. (2015, March 18). Half the money I spend on advertising is wasted; the trouble is I don't know which half. Retrieved from https://www.b2bmarketing.net/en/resources/blog/half-money-i-spend-advertising-wasted-trouble-i-dont-know-which-half?currency=USD

delegated, but you *have to* review the harvested data no matter what. For instance, when scoping out your competition's funnels in Chapter 6, either tackle it solo or work with the person who implements your funnels and marketing. It's incredibly valuable for you to go through this process yourself so you can experience it.

CHAPTER 5

YOUR TARGET MARKET

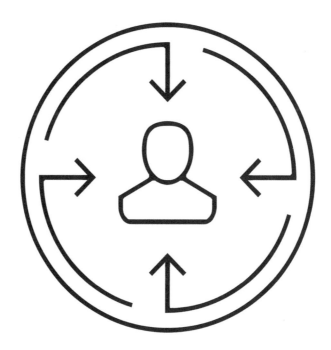

Customers are the lifeblood of your business. Without them, you don't have a business. Therefore, it's safe to say that you should take care of them, but how well do you actually know them?

At my workshops and events I often ask ecom business owners, "Who is your target audience?" I get answers like, "People who like fishing," or "Women who do yoga." If this is how you define your target market and what you base your marketing efforts on, I can guarantee that your business is struggling.

What would be a better answer? If you have a yoga brand, I would love to hear that your target market is white-collared, married women over the age of 40 who drive a Lexus, BMW, or Mercedes; have two school-age children; and have turned to yoga to help deal with stress and get their bodies back in shape.

Yes, you have to be that specific. Of those two audiences (one vague and the other granular), which would be easier to effectively target with a marketing campaign? If you were creating sales copy, who would you be able to create an effective message for? That's why being specific is so important.

Less than a handful of the people I ask this question to give me an adequately detailed answer and the reason is because most businesses only have a surface-level impression of who their customers are. They may think their customers are simply people who like yoga, mountain biking, or in my case, guns. But that's not knowing your customer; that is making an unfounded assumption.

Knowing your customers shows in everything your business does, and your customers will be able to see and appreciate that. The more you learn about them, the less money you waste and the fewer issues you have selling your products. That helps with brand loyalty, repeat purchases, and all kinds of additional secondary perks. It makes your customers think of your business, not as just another store, but as something to be excited and passionate about.

Gathering intricate data about your customers takes a lot of time and work, which is why it's often neglected. But trust me, knowing your demographic is worth the effort because it makes it easier to pinpoint where to advertise, who to target, what to sell them, and how to sell it to them.

Ultimately, this chapter is about getting so deep into customer demographics, social data, and behavioral data that you can build a customer avatar–a perfect picture of your ideal customer. When you use this customer avatar to help you make business decisions, you'll find that everything starts to fall into place and fit together in a more cohesive way.

Remember, you may be a consumer within your market, but you're *not* your market. The second you decide to go into business and sell, you now have a completely different thought process from the consumer. It may be a minor perception shift, but you'll think about things differently.

A new decision or product idea may sound great to you and your team, but would your customers like it? Would your *avatar* like it? Asking yourself that question can steer you away from tons of disastrous decisions.

As Nathan Furr and Paul Ahlstrom say in their book *Nail It Then Scale It*, "Which would you rather do–talk to customers now and find you're wrong or talk to customers in a year and thousands of dollars down the road and still find out you're wrong?"[23] Talk to them now, learn who they are, and you'll thank yourself in a year–and for many years to come.

Demographics

Merriam Webster defines demographics as "the quantifiable statistics of a given population," but in terms of

---

[23] Wagner, Eric T. (2013, September 12). Five reasons 8 out of 10 businesses fail. Retrieved from http://www.forbes.com/sites/ericwagner/2013/09/12/five-reasons-8-out-of-10-businesses-fail/#61fbdb585e3c

ecommerce, customer demographics are a little more specific than that. They're *the generalized character traits shared by the people who buy your products.*

There are a number of key demographic data points to consider:

Customer Demographics

- **Age**. What age or age range are your target market in? Typically, you will find that 80% of your customers come from a very specific age range.

- **Location**. Where do the live?

- **Gender**. Every business usually attracts more of one gender than the other. Who does your business attract?

- **Race and ethnicity**. This is good thing to know for marketing and targeting your products.

- **Household income**. How much do they earn? Single income or combined?

- **Homeownership status**. Do they rent or have a mortgage? Do they live in a house, duplex, apartment, or condo?

- **Disabilities**. Does your target market have a disability, health issue, or are they prone to developing one down the road?

- **Education**. What is their education level? You may find that the best demographic for your business are people with master's degrees, or a Bachelor of Arts instead of a Bachelor of Science.

- **Employment**. Are they employed? What kind of job do they have?

- **Children**. Do they have kids? If so, how many? How old are they?

- **Marital status**. Are they married? Divorced? Separated? Single?

- **Political affiliation**. Do they identify with a particular party? How strongly? Do they vote? What political issues are important to them?

When you collect demographic information on your customers, what you're really doing is hunting for data clusters. Data clusters form when you combine your customer demographics and your market demographics. They can tell you that 85 percent of your customers are women, 52 percent of those women are Caucasian, and 36 percent of those Caucasian women are homeowners.

There are people who say, "my market is women!" when their market is really a subset of the female demographic. With today's marketing technology, you can target anyone, no matter how complicated the niche. And guess what? The more criteria you add, the more specific your marketing can get.

Ezra Firestone, the owner of a company called Boom and a good friend of mine, has shown me his impressive statistics (he makes $1.5 million per month in gross revenue, and is on track to make $20 million by the end of 2016). Boom sells all kinds of makeup for women, but it specifically targets women over 40. The brand encourages women to embrace their age and make the most of it instead of trying to hide it.[24]

It's a great company that's growing at a ridiculous rate, but without the necessary data points they wouldn't have targeted the right demographic. There's a specific type of woman who identifies with Boom, and you can bet Ezra knows exactly who she is. Some of Boom's additional data key points may tie into

---

[24] Thoughts. (n.d.). Retrieved from
http://www.boombycindyjoseph.com/pages/thoughts

education level, marital status, political affiliation—Ezra would have never known until he saw the data.

The point is, it's crazy just how specific you can get. Eliminating data just because you don't think it's important can have detrimental effects on your marketing efforts, and that's always dangerous.

Depending on your niche, some of these data points may not be important. Even so, it's always a good idea to know all of them. Even if half of the data points on this list don't play a big role in your business, they can still give you information you didn't know or expect and that can give you an edge in crafting your marketing messages.

Let's say you don't care if your customers own or rent a home because you sell fitness supplements, but you check anyway and your market research shows that 75 percent of your customers own homes. That's a good thing to know, because it can help narrow down your targeting and also tells you that your customers are more 'established' in life than you may have otherwise suspected. You can now test advertising that specifically targets homeowners that meet your other criteria and exclude renters. Marketing tests like this are how you stumble across your sweet spot audiences that generate your biggest profits.

Tools for Finding Audience Data

Since you need customer information to use the following tools, it helps to export your own customer data beforehand. Once you have your data, keep in mind that no single one of the tools in this section gives you enough data to know your market—you have to use multiple tools and combine the data. I used to do this busywork myself, but now I only do it if we are diving into a new market. Otherwise, I have an employee do it, but I always make sure to review the information afterwards.

Facebook Insights

One of the easiest ways to get demographic information is through Facebook Insights. If you run a fan page for your business, you can use the "insights" tab to gather data on the people who like your page—who they are, what kind of pages they like, their age ranges, their marital status, etc. All of this information is available to you as the owner, and it's all free.

You can also find out which hours of the day your customers are most active on Facebook. You can use that to time your advertising to match peak activity times so you get the most bang for your buck. Looking at the insights of your fans is a good place to start, but to leverage Facebook's insights to the max, you should upload your customer lists and let Facebook match up your customers to their Facebook profiles.

Facebook Audience Insights

To use Facebook Audience Insights fully, you have to upload lists of your customers' email addresses and phone numbers to Facebook. If you have both the email and phone number, use both because some people match on just the email or just the phone number. In my experience, 50 to 60 percent of customer emails and 70 percent of phone numbers usually match up when uploaded to Facebook.

Facebook Audience Insights matches the emails and phone numbers that you upload to user profiles. It then tells you the composition of your audience, including customer demographics. These are exact demographics that make up who your existing customers are, which makes them incredibly valuable, because now you know exactly who to target to find more customers like them.

Facebook Audience Insights won't just say if someone is single or married; it will tell you if someone is in a relationship or married but separated. It won't just say if someone has a college degree; it will tell you what type of degree they have, it can tell you if they are currently in school, and which school they are attending. It tells you which brands and groups people have liked on Facebook too. Facebook Audience Insights can even offer guesses about the types of vehicles people might be shopping for based on their history.

TowerData

TowerData is a big data company that aggregates data from thousands of sources. They have information on almost everybody because they are a data-append service. This means that, like Facebook Insights, you give them some customer data and they match it with other data. You give them a phone number and they try to match it to a name, address, credit cards, home ownership, associations, subscriptions, etc. Every time they find a match, that profile gets a little more detailed.

TowerData claims on their website that they can match up to 80 percent of your list with exact data on your customer.[25] If they make a match, they'll return all of that information to you. Not only will they give you the information for that particular person, they'll also give you the overall statistical information

---

[25] Enhance your email list with email intelligence. Tower Data. Retrieved from http://www.towerdata.com/email-intelligence/email-enhancement

in a neat, compiled report that you can use to make smarter decisions in your marketing.

Twitter Analytics

You may know Twitter for its annoying celebrity rants, but Twitter also makes a massive amount of data and analytics available to users. If you use Twitter for marketing and have a large Twitter following, you can pull up the analytics data from your followers and see all kinds of different demographic information about your customers, prospects, and target market. Twitter is very underutilized as a research tool because its data interface is not as user friendly as it could be, but there are a number of tools on the market that can help you mine the Twitter data more effectively. One of my favorites is listed in the member's area of BuildGrowScale.com.

Alexa

Alexa, which has been around since 1996, provides analytics and commercial web traffic data that helps you analyze traffic on websites. It can give you a ton of good demographic information about your general market that you can then use to better locate your ideal customer. To use it, just put in URLs for sites that fit your market and see what data it returns.

If you use Alexa to research the sites your market frequents, you can learn a lot. For example, if you have a cooking site, you could plug in Betty Crocker and discover that Betty Crocker's customers also frequent Southern Living Magazine, Pampered Chef, and Martha Stewart. Maybe you had no idea that your customers liked Southern Living, and now you can take advantage of that knowledge in your marketing.

Alexa also tells you what percentage of people go from the Betty Crocker site to the Southern Living site (and many other patterns). If you plug in your competitor's information, you can learn key information about them and their traffic as well.

Google Analytics

Google Analytics is great on the advertising front, so you **have to** have it installed on your website and also use the special tracking and tagging code in your links. It gives you data about everyone who visits your site, even people who aren't customers. Over time, this data will build up and you can start pinpointing interesting data clusters that will give you even more insight into your market.

Survey

Surveys are one of the simplest ways to get information from your customers. Send customers a survey containing a few questions with multiple choice answers and you can get information directly from the source.

Social and Behavior Data

Demographics tell you who, where, and what, but you won't know any of the hows or whys. You might have a customer's name, employment, and age, but you still don't know who they are. So once you have basic customer demographic information, it's time to learn what really makes your ideal customers tick.

You only have a one-dimensional view, and you need to make a three-dimensional profile of your ideal customer. The next step is to get behavioral and social information that will help you get a more complete picture of your customer. To do that, find the answers to all of the following questions; each one helps you further understand your consumer base.

Social and Behavioral Data

- **Leisure activities**. What do they do for fun? What are their hobbies?

- **Sites frequented**. What kinds of sites do they frequent?

- **Five favorite niche influencers**. Who are the top five niche influencers your customers follow? Niche influencers are the influential "celebrities" of your market's niche. For example, if you're in the Bikram Yoga market, the niche influencers might be popular Bikram Yoga bloggers or podcasters. Niche influencers can affect how people perceive your product because people care about the niche influencer's opinions.

- **Favorite podcasts**. Which podcasts in your market do they listen to? What topics do they focus on?

- **Preferred social networks**. What social networks and forums do they frequent?

- **Technology proficiency**. Are they computer literate, or are they more like my hunting demographic (so outdoorsy that they only use a computer when they have to and they don't enjoy it when they do)?

- **Content consumption**. How do they like to consume content? Audio? Video? Written? Big chunks or bite sized pieces?

- **Online shopping frequency**. How frequently do they shop online, and when they do shop online, how do they search for products? Are they search shoppers, comparison-site shoppers, or referral shoppers?

- **Price tolerance**. This is generally based on income levels. Are they depression-era people who always snatch up a good deal because their circumstances pre-conditioned them to do so? Or are they much more focused on sales because they have a limited disposable income? Or does price not matter and they just buy whatever catches their fancy?

- **Interpersonal skills**. Are they loners or joiners? This is important for creating a community; you don't want to repel your loner customers. It'll tell you if it's better to take a "solidarity" approach to marketing instead of an "us" approach.

Tools for Finding Social and Behavioral Data

Looking for the answers? These tools will help you find the social and behavioral data you need. Just like the tools for finding demographics, any single tool won't give you as complete of a picture as using all four methods (like I do) will. I know this is a manual process, but it's an effective way to learn what makes your market tick, and that knowledge will pay off, I promise.

Facebook

The best way to find social demographics is through Facebook Insights. Unlike when we used Facebook Insights to spy on our customers before, now we're focusing on the social demographics of the market your customers live in and how they behave within that market. Facebook Insights links to other interest pages and groups, so if you join some relevant Facebook groups and start using Facebook Insights, you can learn what makes these people tick online (what they're consuming, clicking on, and liking).

You can also browse Facebook pages related to your niche and harvest data from other interest pages and groups. Just check fan pages for niches, companies, and celebrity public profiles, pull all that into Facebook Insights, and start filtering through the data. Getting into groups, interacting with people, and reading their posts and shares can also answer a ton of questions.

Niche Magazines

Magazines.com lists thousands of magazines for every market imaginable. Subscribe to the magazines that target your niche, and read those magazines so you know what your demographic is interested in. As an added bonus, you can plug the magazine websites into Alexa to find out even more about your demographic. Also when it comes to figuring out what to say and how to market to your audience, go to a bookstore with a large magazine rack. Pull a bunch of the magazines that fit your niche and look at their covers, the images, and the sales language they use. I assure you it is all premeditated and deliberate; what you see is what works for your market.

Google

You probably use Google all the time, but the trick to using it to find social and behavioral data is to type in your niche name followed by "+ forums." If your niche is mixed martial arts, for example, type in "mixed martial arts + forums." Join relevant online forums, read the posts, join in the discussions, and find out what your customer wants.

SimilarWeb

If you ignore everything else in this section, don't ignore SimilarWeb. Plug all of your competitor sites and other sites your niche frequents into it, and it returns a massive amount of data on what the market is doing, who they are, how they are acting, what they are consuming, where they come from, and more. It's great for getting a lot of data at once and it's data you won't find elsewhere without a lot of digging.

Your Customer Avatar

When you know somebody well, you can get them to do anything you want (within reason). Think of a close relative or good friend of yours; you know that person on an intimate level, so you know what to say or how to phrase something to get what you want from them.

Now imagine being able to do that with customers that you've never met, and being able to do it online. *That's what knowing your customers does for your ecommerce business.*

Nestled within all the customer information you've collected is a subsection of data that reveals your dream (ideal) customer. Using all the data points collected, you can find clusters and build that profile. That's what we're trying to get to: your customer avatar.

A customer avatar is the persona of your ideal buyer. It's a tool that sharpens your ability to successfully generate and keep customers. When you have a solid avatar, you'll know exactly what to say, what to offer, where to advertise, and how to create your marketing materials to not only attract that ideal customer, but convert them into a buyer.

I create a customer avatar in every one of my businesses. I won't launch a business or spend any money until a customer avatar is developed.

I first heard about the concept in a seminar many years ago, but it was one of my mentors who made me take the time to do the market research and create a customer avatar the way I describe in this section. Before that, I had an extremely generic view of my customer and I was spending too much money on marketing. My sales letters and copy were written in extremely broad language because I was trying to speak to a huge audience.

Once I built an avatar, my businesses transformed. I wasn't targeting a broad audience anymore; I was speaking to one person. I wrote my copy and product descriptions the same way I would talk to that one person, and it changed my whole business.

Everything is more congruent now. There's no breakage in my brand message because everything—my ads, site design, the landing page, the upsells, and the checkout process—is designed specifically for my customer avatar. When I'm having a meeting or a scrum session at the office, I make one of my assistants play (pretend to be) the avatar and become a point of contention. My team and I can "talk" to the avatar and make sure that any new decision matches what our avatar wants.

In this section, I'll give you four steps you can use to create your own customer avatar. Once you've created the avatar, put them on a spreadsheet, format it nicely, add a picture and all the details, and print it out. Stick it over your desk as a constant reminder of your ideal customer.

Of course, this tool isn't just for you. Give a copy of your avatar to everyone on your staff. Give it to anyone you outsource branding, design, etc., and tell them to keep the avatar in mind when doing their work.

Use the avatar whenever you're working on branding, composing newsletters, designing products, writing sales copy, creating ads, posting on social media, or crafting marketing campaigns. Do everything with your customer avatar in mind, and your business will transform just like mine did.

1. Demographics

First, assemble the baseline for your avatar: your basic demographic data. Figure out the perfect age, gender, income level, and education of your customer. Depending on your market, you may also want to include whether or not your perfect customer owns a home.

2. The Seven Emotional Questions

After you pull that basic information, start adding your customer's wants and needs. You can do that by answering the seven emotional questions about your customer.

I usually put these questions in a spreadsheet and fill in the answers using the social and behavioral data from earlier. To answer these seven questions, use your research from forums, Facebook groups, and similar resources. People tell their stories on those sites.

What's the commonality of all these stories? You are trying to figure out, not who all of your customers are, but who that one perfect customer is. You can use the answers to these questions to piece together your avatar.

The Seven Emotional Questions

A. What are they thinking and feeling?

B. What are they being told about your products and market?

C. What are they being told in the marketplace?

D. As a consumer, what do they see when they look at your niche?

E. What can they gain from your market?

F. What are their fears about the market and niche?

G. What do they want to achieve within this market, and why is it important to them?

3. The Ten Behavioral Questions

These questions are designed to help you flesh out your avatar. We're creating a character, a real person you can have a "conversation" with. I recommend you put these questions and answers in that spreadsheet you made for the previous section.

A. **What's their name?** Give your customer avatar a name to make it feel real. If you are doing this right, the name should be tough to come up with.

B. **What do they look like?** Give them characteristics. Are they fat, tall, short, skinny? Do they have acne? Do they wear glasses?

C. **Where do they live?** Which country do they live in? Do they live in the city or the suburbs? Does your avatar live in a house, a condo, or an apartment? Do they like where they live?

D. **What's their profession and where do they work?** Are they white or blue collar? Are they happy with their work or would they like to change it?

E. **Who do they associate with?** Do they belong to any groups, clubs, or associations? Who are they friends with?

F. **What's their marital status?** Are they happily married, separated, divorced? If they aren't married, do they want to get married?

G. **How many kids do they have, if any?** How old are the kids? What gender?

H. **What roadblocks in life brought them to this market or made them more receptive to it?** This is particularly important if your products deal with health, wealth, or beauty.

I. **What are they good at?** What do they excel at that makes them special or unique?

J. **What are they bad at?** Do they know they are bad at them? Does it embarrass them? What are they doing about it?

4. Create a Background Story

Now, combine the information from steps one through three and create a story for your avatar. I usually pretend (and this is what I teach my students) that I'm back in school and writing a story for English class. You're trying to write a story, so if it helps, start with, "once upon a time…" you can always edit that out later.

Start with the easy stuff: age, marital status, sex, number of children, employment, etc. Use that as a foundation for the more emotional aspects of the story. As you create the story of your avatar, you become more involved and your subconscious will learn to read the character the same way it does a good friend.

Once you've written the story, match a face to it. Attaching a picture of a person to the story makes it feel real. Use stock photography sites or try a site like Uifaces.com, where you can get avatar images of people free of charge. Finding the right picture can be hard–it's always been tough for me–but that's a good thing because it means you're invested in your avatar and know what they look like.

Once that's done, take a step back. The first draft is never a home run. Read your story, look at the picture, then pour over your research, reevaluate the different demographics as well as the questions that you answered, and reread the story again. Does the avatar you built match the data? If not, keep revising until it's a perfect match.

Example of a Customer Avatar

Mark is a 30-year-old go-getter. He's a full-time HR manager for a large software company in Austin, Texas. He's married to his high school sweetheart, Julie, and together they have a beautiful eight-month-old baby girl.

Mark works 50+ hour weeks at his job and though he doesn't really enjoy it, he's willing to work so that Julie can stay home with their daughter. The downside is that, while he's very grateful to have a job in this economy, he feels like his daughter is growing up without him.

That's why Mark has been burning the midnight oil for the last six months, trying to crack the code to making money online so he can quit his job and work from home. Mark has realistic goals and knows he's not going to make millions overnight, but he still finds it hard to keep the hope of replacing his $50,000 annual income alive when nothing he tries produces a worthwhile result. He's been racking up credit card debt buying business course after business course, only to find out that the only money those courses make is for the person selling them.

Julie is trying to be supportive, but she doesn't understand Mark's decision; all she sees is the growing credit card bills and the long hours Mark spends on the computer. They now spend more time arguing than talking, and it's taking a toll on both of them. In an effort to make peace, Mark has promised Julie that if the online thing doesn't work after just one more try, he'll give up his dreams and come back to her reality.

Mark is in overdrive now and determined to make working from home a viable option. After all of his trial and errors, he knows what doesn't work and that what he needs to do is create and sell his own information products online. He has several ideas for good products, he just needs a proven and workable plan.

Can You Have More Than One Customer Avatar?

Some businesses realize over time that there's more than one customer avatar that fits their business model. That's fine, but making multiple customer avatars is only necessary if you have strong statistical data that shows your target market has large groups of customers in extremely different categories.

You may find you have fairly equal sales between both men and women. In that case, your business needs two avatars, and each avatar is bound to have a unique emotional and behavioral profile. Men and women do not think about things the same way right? Or maybe your customers have a significant age gap. Let's say your core customers are men between the ages of 35 to 55. The thought process of a 35-year-old and a 55-year-old man is completely different, so you'll need to split your demographic into two groups and develop separate avatars for both age groups.

Multiple customer avatars are possible, but it's hard to manage more than three. Every avatar requires its own complete marketing channel, criteria, branding, elements, image, etc., and it would be extremely difficult to maintain more than three of them.

Can You Use a Real Customer Instead of an Avatar?

Sure, if you have an actual customer who fits your ideal customer model, you can use them instead of an avatar. However, keep in mind that your customer avatar often evolves as you get more customers and acquire more data. You may start out with Jerry, but after a year you may need a Larry, and you'll have to reevaluate. You can't do that with a real person; you can only do it with an avatar.

Conclusion

After reading this chapter, you're probably thinking that this is a lot of work. It *is* a lot of work, but again, business is a lot of work. I've never liked making customer avatars, but I know it's important, so I'm willing to commit the time to make an avatar without shortcutting the process.

Doing the research, finding customer details, and developing a customer profile lets you make better decisions, waste less money, make more money, and ultimately have a less stressful time in business. If you're trying to develop a sales message for a group, you lose people. It's only when you speak one person that you connect.

You'll *speak* to your target market once you have a customer avatar. If you look at the customer avatar as a way to connect with your customers, you'll be ten times more successful.

Chapter 5 Summary

Do the necessary market research to know your customers and your competition. It may not be fun, but you have to push yourself to do it if you want to be successful.

Use tools like Facebook Insights, Facebook Audience Insights, TowerData, Google Analytics, Twitter Analytics, and Alexa to find key data about your target demographic.

Use tools like Facebook, Google, SimilarWeb, and niche magazines to gather social and behavioral data on your demographic.

Create a customer avatar that represents your ideal customer using the demographics and social and behavioral data you collected. Create a story and find a picture for your avatar so they feel real to you and your staff, then make all your business decisions based on the needs of that avatar.

CHAPTER 6

YOUR COMPETITION

I used to barely pay attention to my competition. I thought it didn't matter what anybody else was doing as long as I did my thing. Most ecom brands are like that; they look at competitive intelligence as just a benchmark, a measuring stick to see how they're doing in relation to their competition.

Sure, competitive intelligence can be used that way, but the reality is that competitive intelligence is *a platform you can use to grow your business.* You can use it to gauge the marketplace and identify areas where you can compete while deepening your understanding of your industry. You can see where your competition is doing well (especially the juggernauts of your niche) and get intelligence on what works. Tracking your competitors also helps you generate marketing ideas and makes your business stand out.

You could easily double the size of your company if you learn just one thing from your competitors. What's working for businesses like yours? Where are they running their ads? How are they doing their campaigns? Is there an area they are neglecting that you can scoop up traffic from? The answers to any one of these questions can greatly benefit your business, but only if you bother to do the research!

Even a couple of years ago, some of this data wasn't available. Today its right at your fingertips, and you're missing out if you don't seize it. You don't have to do all this research yourself, but you *do* have to get it done somehow and use it to your advantage.

Once you get through this chapter and learn how to gather a large amount of intelligence (as well as what that data tells you about the market and how you can compete), you'll be kicking yourself for not knowing all of this sooner. When you have the data on what's actually working, you don't have to guess anymore. You'll know what works and you can immediately apply it to your business.

Find Your Biggest Competitors

To kick off your competitor research, you need to find the top five to ten competitors in your target market. I don't mean the giant brands of the world; I mean your specific niche competition.

I strive to find ten competitors for each of my businesses. I may have to stretch to call some of them direct competitors, but the idea is to find my target market and get a complete set of data. If you're in a low-competition niche, you may struggle to find even five competitors, while if you're in a hyper-competitive niche you may have trouble narrowing your list down to ten. It's not bad to have more than ten competitors for your research, but keep in mind that it makes research more time consuming.

How to Find Your Competitors

There are three simple ways to find your competitors. Complete these steps in the following order for best results.

1. Google

There are keywords that directly apply to every specific market. Think of what you believe are the top ten keywords for your market, or use a keyword tool like WordRecon to help you assemble a list of your top keywords. Once you've done that, run searches for your primary keywords on Google to root out your competition.

You should look for two things. First, **find organic ranked competitors**. On the first page you may find a few sites that don't count as competitors, including sites like About.com or WebMD.com (content sites that don't sell anything). Ignore these, go two or three pages deep, and find the competitors that sell physical products.

Second, **look for paid advertisements on Google or AdWords** that use your various keywords. You may have to go several pages deep to find enough relevant ads because they're only placed at the top and the bottom of the search page.

Write down the names and URLs of the five to ten top competitors you find through these two methods (you only need one list). You'll dig deeper into this list later and find out who your true competitors are.

Some markets may not have many companies running paid ads, and that's okay. But if most of your keywords don't have any paid ads, beware. This means that either your competition hasn't discovered that keyword or that the keyword doesn't monetize well. If there are significant competitors in your market and they're not spending money on that keyword, there's usually a reason why.

2. SEMrush

Everyone who tracks Google rankings uses SEMrush. It's a paid tool, and it's not cheap, but it's totally worth the money if you want comprehensive data. There's a free version that works fine for this type of research as well, and if you discover that you want deeper data, you can always spring for the paid version later.

I use SEMrush to flush out additional competitors, eliminate a lot of non-competitors, and get more granular data on everyone as a whole. There are many kinds of search options on SEMrush, and most of them are very advanced, but you should stick to the organic search for competitors.

First, input the biggest competitor you found in your Google research. SEMrush will then tell you who the biggest competitors are for that site in terms of number of keywords. For example, if you input marthastewart.com, SEMrush could tell you that Betty Crocker and Southern Living are Martha Stewart's biggest competitors based on the number of keywords.

Collect the top competitors from the search before running a search for the next competitor on the Google list. Once you've run all your original competitors through SEMrush, you'll build up a fairly sizable list of sites (usually 15 to 30).

You'll find that some sites you thought were competitors aren't competitors at all just by collecting this data, since they won't show up in the SEMrush search results. Finally, SEMrush can bring new keywords to your attention because it generates a number of keywords that relate to each site you run a search for.

3. Alexa

Once you've completed the first two steps, plug each competitor on your new and improved list into Alexa to get even deeper data. Alexa is one of the oldest data aggregators, and it gives useful information like:

- The global traffic ranking of your competitors

- The number of websites that link back to sites (back-linking)

- The type of searches that drive people to those websites

- Audience demographics that give you a picture of your competitor's target demographic (compare it to the demographics data you collected per the previous chapter)

- Site load time. How long does it take your competitor's website to load?

Collect information like this on every big competitor site and use it to start building a profile. I take screenshots of the information and put it into a spreadsheet to make sure I remember everything.

The Three Steps to Find Your Competition

1. **Google**. Figure out your market's top ten keywords (or use a tool like WordRecon) and search for them on Google. Make a list of five to ten competitors derived from your top ten organic ranked competitors and from advertisers who use your keywords on Google AdWords.
2. **SEMrush**. Do an organic research search on each competitor on your list from Step 1. Add new competitors from the SEMrush search results until you have a list of 15 to 30 competitors.
3. **Alexa**. Search for each competitor using Alexa to get deep data including load time, audience demographics, and back-linking. Use this information to create a profile for each competitor.

Document How Each Competitor Operates

You should now have a decent list of competitors, including competitors you likely never knew existed before. It's time to get a feel of who they are and how they operate on the surface level.

This is something most businesses don't take the time to go through in great detail. They kind of glance at their competitors and move on, even though getting surface-level information is so simple and a little time on a competitor's website gives you a massive amount of useful information.

There are all kinds of little things you can do to stand out from the competition while giving your customer a better experience. These tiny differences can boost your conversions, get you more sales, increase your average cart value, and make your customers happier. Each thing you notice your competitor doing wrong may lead you to tweak your business, and these little tweaks can accumulate to big changes.

As you analyze your competitors, look for their pros and cons, places where they're not maximizing, and any gaps in the market that they're not fulfilling. Also note the similarities they have with your business. Assimilate all this data into a spreadsheet (make a column for each question) so you can quickly look at each competitor and see any trends, patterns, or gaps that pop up in the data.

When I complete this step, I always notice simple but important things about my competitors. Once, while doing this research, that one of my biggest competitors in the fitness niche was not mobile optimized at all. I initially thought they were kicking butt on mobile because I saw their ads on mobile all the time, but when I pulled up their site up on my phone, looked at their product, and added it to the cart, I realized it was terrible. I couldn't even get the checkout to work!

I knew that if this business were focused so heavily on mobile optimization and running this much traffic, they either didn't have a clue what they were doing and were wasting money OR they were still making a lot of money on mobile conversions despite their subpar mobile optimization. Considering the size of the company, I knew they weren't stupid enough to lose money, which meant they were profitable despite their lackluster mobile performance.

Because of this, I realized if I mobile optimized my business and targeted mobile users, I could make a lot of money (as per Principle 9). Sure enough, when we got everything mobile optimized, we saw a 15 percent lift in mobile sales, and once we dialed in our mobile advertising we had a 28 percent boost in overall sales. This is just one example of the many ways doing competitor research has sharpened my businesses.

Competitor Research Checklist

What does their branding say about them? Look at their brand and infer its message. Are they like GoPro, with a specific market (extreme sports and outdoors), or are they like Walmart, with no distinct market and nothing to offer but cheap prices?

How do they communicate their value proposition? What angles do they use to position their products? Are the products made in the U.S.? Handcrafted? Military grade? Luxury? What hooks—emotional pulls—do they use to pique your interest in the product? Do they use fear? Sense of belonging? Status? Pain?

What are their prices like? Are they a premium-price, middle ground, or bargain competitor? How do they present their prices? For instance, if they are expensive, do they seem apologetic or confident about it?

How do they present their products? Do they have a bestseller list or a "feature products" list on their product page? Does the positioning match the price? Does the packaging enhance or hurt the product, and does it fit with the brand message they are trying to send?

What kind of photos do they use? Do they have great product photos with a lot of different angles or do they use basic stock photos?

What's the layout of their product page? Is it conducive to sales or is it choppy? Do they incorporate videos and reviews? Does it have "buy" buttons all over the place?

How do they handle shipping? Are their shipping rates higher or lower than yours? What are their shipping options? Are they a one-trick pony or do they offer multiple options like free shipping, discount shipping, or upgraded shipping?

Is their sales pitch aggressive or passive? Does it feel like you're being sold heavily or does it feel friendly and laid back? Or alternatively, does it feel like they're not asking for the sale strongly enough?

What kind of call to action do they use? How are they asking for the sale? If they use buttons, what color and type are the buttons? Are they "add to cart" or "buy now" buttons? Where have they placed buy buttons, and how does it compare to where you've placed yours?

Do they have any default promotions or incentives? You may notice that some sites do promotions like "buy two get one free" indefinitely. No business wastes site space running a promotion that's not converting, so when you see these promotions, you can often duplicate them and find an easy win. Document these promotions and pay special attention to whether the competitor is using the promotion for list building. Are they offering a coupon or a lead magnet in exchange for an email?

Is the site and checkout optimized for mobile devices? Pull up their site on your smartphone, add a product to cart, and look at their checkout. Is it functional with a nice display, or is it hard to use?

What's their social media presence like? Do they use Facebook, YouTube, Twitter, or Pinterest? Do they interact with their fans and customers? Do they seem heavily engaged or does it look dead?

Do they do any content marketing? Do they have a blog where they write articles or post videos? Do they link to content relevant to their products?

Reverse-Engineer Your Competition

At this point, you've likely determined the major players in your market. You can eliminate companies that are not your true competitors (based on what they sell and who their audiences are) and focus on the right businesses.

Your shortlist should consist of five to ten competitors. Assemble them in order of importance, and then get ready to reverse engineer your biggest competitors through some good old-fashioned snooping.

As I mentioned in this chapter's introduction, you couldn't find any of this data just a few years ago. The technology either wasn't there or so underground that only a few people knew how to sniff it out, but now there are a bunch of tools that you can use to reverse-engineer your competition. I'll teach you about some of the tools that show you exactly what your competition is doing and how they're doing it. You'll discover what's working and how to pull out the gems that make your competition so successful. Use these tools in order for the best results.

1. SEMrush

Does this look familiar? It's the tool you used to find new competitors. Now we'll use it to find two other pieces of information.

First, plug in the competitors on your shortlist and find out which top-performing keywords each competitor ranks number one for. For example, if you're in the kitchen accessories niche, you may find out that Betty Crocker ranks number one for the keywords "nonstick spatula" and "heat-resistant spatula." This helps lay the foundation for the search optimization strategy you'll use for your store. If you're making a content marketing plan, find out which of those keywords generates the most traffic for your competition.

Second, use SEMrush's incredible pay-per-click research function to dissect your competitors' AdWords campaigns. AdWords is a tough nut to crack; it costs thousands of dollars to buy traffic, test, tweak, and find the high-performing keywords and ad creatives that work best. SEMrush actually delivers a blueprint of the AdWords campaigns your competitors are running in the form of *a full PDF report of the campaign*, with a complete breakdown of your competition's AdWords advertising data.

I **cannot stress enough** how valuable this data is. You can use it to duplicate your competitors' successful campaigns instead of spending the time and money to build your own from the ground up. From there, you can test and tweak the campaign until it's working optimally for your business.

2. BuzzSumo

After you've done your keyword research using SEMrush, plug the highest-ranked keywords into BuzzSumo. BuzzSumo is a research tool that tells you what content is popular on the web and where it's shared. It shows you what kind of content your audience is consuming based on your primary keywords.

When you input a keyword into BuzzSumo, it returns a list of the top content related to that keyword, including links to source websites. It also provides data on how many times content has been shared globally on platforms like Facebook, Twitter, Pinterest, LinkedIn, and Google Plus. BuzzSumo can also rank the results by total shares or social reach and show you how your market is interacting on different social platforms.

Basically, BuzzSumo tells you which social media platforms your business can do well on so you can focus on the platforms where your content will have the strongest impact. If a social platform like Pinterest or Twitter doesn't have a lot of hits for you, it means your audience doesn't use those networks and you shouldn't bother with them.

3. WhatRunsWhere

WhatRunsWhere searches the web for massive amounts of paid advertising data on your competitors. This is priceless data if you use paid media to grow your business, and as you know from Principle 8, paid media is critical to the success of an ecommerce business.

Run a WhatRunsWhere search on each one of your top competitors and you can get a complete picture of the business from the campaign level down to the ad level, the targeting, and, finally, the landing page. You can see how it all flows together and observe what's working and what's not.

WhatRunsWhere also tells you how long the business has been running (and paying for) a particular ad campaign. The longer an ad has been running, the higher the chance is that it's profitable. After all, nobody runs an unprofitable campaign for very long.

4. SimilarWeb

SimilarWeb gives you tons of information about your competitors. It reveals traffic referral sites, top destination sites, social traffic breakdowns, and banner ads, and you can leverage all of this data to make some key changes in your business.

First, you can use SimilarWeb to find the sites that refer the most traffic to your competitor. This isn't necessarily paid traffic; your competitor could be getting a lot of their traffic from unpaid sources like About.com, Yahoo! Answers, or Huffington Post.

Either way, once you know the sites referring this traffic, your next step is to find the top destination sites. Where do people go after they leave your competitor's website? SimilarWeb reveals statistical data clusters that show the websites your audience frequents, which shows you more websites you can advertise on. If your target audience is going from a competitor's site to other niche sites, you could buy paid advertising on those sites.

SimilarWeb also shows social traffic breakdowns. Where does your competitor's traffic on social media come from?

What platform do they leverage the most and how frequently? Each competitor has a slightly different breakdown for all of this data, but you can build a fuller picture of your market when you use SimilarWeb.

The other thing that's really awesome about SimilarWeb is that it reveals what kind of banner ads your competitor is using, and which ones are getting the most clicks. You may also find that people who click on your competitor's sites also click on other banner ads, which can lead to unexpected trends. Everybody who loves your Bikram Yoga products, for example, may also like glucosamine joint medication.

Make note of these trends and look for commonalities. If a large percentage of the people interested in what you sell favor the same items/interests/topics, you can target those interests while you sell your products. You may be able to join forces with affiliates or even start side businesses (if you're that yoga seller, why not branch out into glucosamine joint medication?).

5. Ghostery

Ghostery is a relatively new tool. It's actually a browser extension that lets you look under the hood of a competitor's store. It's easy to install, and all you have to do is activate the extension while on your competitor's website to use it.

Ghostery's function is simple: it makes all the invisible code elements on websites visible. I mostly use it to look at the type of retargeting pixels, tracking codes, and ad network codes (like Bing and Yahoo!) are on a competitor site.

These elements have a specific format, and when Ghostery reveals them, you can see what your competitors use to leverage traffic. Are they using fancy geo-targeting scripts or something similar? You may find data your initial research missed.

Funnel Hack

Now that you've collected all the data you need from your top competitors, it's time for you to become a customer. Yes, I'm telling you to spend money on your competitor's products.

Trying a competitor's products is a great opportunity! Think of it as a low-level form of hacking. You are basically going through your competitor's funnel as a customer and "hacking it apart" to find what's good and bad. You'll then develop your own strategy based on what you learn.

Most people ignore this tactic, while others have never considered buying their competitors' products. Remember that you're not buying products, you're buying *data*. This is priceless data, ESPECIALLY from your most successful competition. Don't think about it as supporting the competitor, think of it as buying data you can't get anywhere else.

You may not know that your customer experience is subpar until you go through somebody else's. Little things like that can have dramatic impacts on your business, but you can only fix them if you're aware of them.

Use this funnel information to rebuild or modify your existing sales process. If your products are similar enough to your competitor's products, you can borrow elements of your competitor's funnel and build your own version. Just run the new funnel head-to-head with your existing funnel to see which one performs better.

How to Execute a Funnel Hack

Use screen recording software to make a video of the entire sales process—you'll want to refer to it later in case you miss something the first time. Take screenshots of the ad, the landing page, the URL, the checkout process, everything. You can never have too many (and they're easier to refer back to than a video).

Start at the ad level. Find an ad offering a product that's similar to what you sell and click on it. Go to the landing page, buy the product, go through the whole process to become a customer.

As you go through their sales funnel, take advantage of everything they suggest. If they have upsells, downsells, or cross-sells, take them. You may have to go through this process multiple times with different products to experience everything your competitor has to offer.

The goal isn't to spend a fortune on your competition; it's to see what's working for them. The better you understand how other businesses operate, the better equipped you'll be to improve your funnels.

It doesn't end there. Most people make the purchase and think it's over, but this is just the initial sales process. You've just become a new customer, and you get to document and learn from everything that comes with it.

- **Emails.** Save the email they send. Make note of how long it takes them to send it, the sequence, and the frequency of emails.

- **Upsells.** Do they immediately try to upsell new products, or do they try to nurture you and build a tighter brand?

- **Retargeting.** Look for retargeting ads. If they don't have any, it's a great opportunity for you because retargeting is one of the best tactics you can employ in a product-based business.

Ordering a competitor's product also gives you a chance to see their actual product. Is it labeled a specific way? What is their packaging like? Is their product better, worse, or comparable to yours? It's one thing to say that your product is the best, but until you've actually purchased your competitors' products, you won't know for sure.

You can return the products afterwards, and doing so is the perfect opportunity to experience your competition's return process. Just remember not to abuse your competition. You're getting something big out of it, so respect them.

After you've funnel-hacked your competitors, you'll know everything about how they operate from the front to the back end. You may even know their business better than they do because you have had the customer experience.

Conclusion

I know researching your competition is an involved process, but it's more than worth it if you pay attention to the data, and it can actually be very interesting. If you find your top five to ten competitors, document how they operate, and learn about their products, marketing strategies, and advertising campaigns, you'll already have more information than most. If you also reverse engineer your competition to the point that you know them better than they know themselves and use what's working for them in your business, you'll likely be outperforming your competition in no time.

Chapter 6 Summary

 Identify your top five to ten competitors using Google, SEMrush, and Alexa (in that order).

 Document how each competitor operates. Look at their pros and cons, and identify any gaps they're leaving in the market.

 Reverse-engineer your competitor and figure out what they are doing and how they're doing it. Become a customer and experience their whole sales process from start to finish, then use your newfound knowledge to ratchet up your own system.

CHAPTER 7

EXPLOIT YOUR DATA

In the past two chapters, you've learned how to micro-analyze your customers and your competition. I've primarily focused on exploiting outside data to improve your company so far, but there's lots of data right in front of you that we have yet to explore.

Very few companies turn their eyes inward towards their sales and customer data. They pull reports on how much they made each month or how many goods they sold.

What if they exploited that data instead, digging through it for information that they could then use to increase their success?

I once worked with a $10 million indie apparel company that had never done any kind of data mining. When I showed them how to organize the data and what to look for, they immediately made several discoveries. They were wasting advertising dollars in some areas while underutilizing advertising dollars in others, and they had a lot of inventory that they kept purchasing even though it wasn't selling.

We immediately did some fire sales to get rid of sunken inventory, recouped advertising cost, and cut down inventory cost. The company became a leaner, more efficient, and more profitable operating machine, and after they tailored their inventory, they saved over a hundred thousand dollars a year and increased overall profits by around 12 percent.

You have a *gold mine* of information in the form of existing customer and transactional data going back as long as your store has been in business. It may not be as relevant if you're a ten-year-old business (what happened in year one is not as important as what happened in the last six months to a year). But if you have any amount of data–a month, two months, three months, five years–you've got a big pile of data that can be used to boost sales and grow your business. That's what this section is all about: learning from the data you already have.

Internal Data Patterns and Analysis

The process of exploiting your data starts with *exporting* your data, and this whole section details the types of data you need to do that. Exporting your sales data is the first and easiest step; everything else in this chapter builds on it.

As discussed in Chapter 5, the process of exporting data depends on your ecommerce platform, so see your platform for details. Whatever platform you're on, export *everything*, not just your last 30 days. For most companies, export no less than six months of data. If you don't have six months of data, work with what you've got.

When you export your data, you may discover that you don't have data on your inventory report or cost of goods because you haven't taken the time to record it or you operate by the seat of your pants. That's a red flag. This data is important, and now is the time to learn why you don't have it and how you can get it. Usually it's built into the platform or your third-party shipper, or it's a manual process with a spreadsheet that you could implement in the office.

Once you have the data, it's game time. You can start immediately improving your company through basket analysis, sales forecasting, inventory forecasting, channel analysis, customer analysis, and your buyer's list. Let's go through these one at a time.

Basket Analysis

In my Second Amendment business, order notifications come in via emails or text alerts. The summaries show the number of purchased items and a sales total. We get tons of those a day, and that's all we see unless we search further and look at what exactly those products were. Unfortunately, most businesses don't bother to do that.

In order to make keeping track of sales easier, some of the big companies record basket history. Platforms keep a log of each time the basket history report is run, so when I start consulting with a lot of these companies, I check out that page mainly to call them out on the fact that they are not doing this. Reviews are usually sporadic, if they even exist.

You know better than that. It's time to look at your sales a little more closely. I want you to look at more than just the sales dollar amounts, revenue, and the amount spent to acquire that revenue.

Sales Data You Need to Know:

- Most consistently selling products
- Best-selling categories
- Items that are most frequently added to carts
- Average cart value

Patterns to Look for:

Poorly-Selling Items

If you fulfill your own products, you're usually aware if a product isn't selling, but if you use a third-party fulfillment center, it's easy to miss. If you have a product that nobody is buying or not enough people are buying, the data always shows it.

Purchase Bundles

What combinations of products are commonly purchased together? Let's say your data shows that people consistently buy yoga mats, yoga towels, and yoga bags together. This data suggests that you could make a yoga bundle—sell these three items together and see if sales go up.

You could even use this information to build funnels. If these three products are frequently purchased together, one of these products can function as a front-end product and the other two can be placed in the upsell sequence of the funnel. If you lower the ticket price of the front-end product, you'll have a good chance of upselling them through the funnel. You can build a whole new customer acquisition funnel based on this data alone.

Best-Selling Products

If you've ever done split testing, you know that the one product you think will shine usually does the worst. You may find that your best-selling products aren't what you thought they would be. If you discover that an ancillary product is your mainstream seller, you should shift focus and drive traffic to it. Why not drive traffic to a product that's selling well, build a landing page for it, and get a higher conversion rate?

Sales Forecasting

Sales forecasting gives you a little peek into the future of your company by using existing data to make revenue projections. There are businesses that assume that if they did $50,000 one month, they'll do $50,000 the next month, but the reality is that all kinds of things happen.

It's hard to grow without forecasts, and you can't forecast if you don't look at your data. There are ebbs and flows to all businesses, and forecasting exposes those ebbs and flows. My businesses often take a pretty significant drop during summer vacation season (June through August). Because I know that, I'm able to plan for that dip.

I do yearly projections, but I focus more on quarterly projections because things change frequently online. Whether you choose an annual or quarterly projection, you should create three forecasts: a conservative forecast, an optimal forecast, and a "shoot for the moon" forecast. You always want your company to grow, so it's important to set different forecasts. If I put the right pieces in place—use the data, restructure, do everything right—I aim for that higher, shoot-for-the-moon forecast. If I fall short, I still end up out-earning my conservative forecast.

When looking at your data for forecasting, go back a year to three years (depending how long your company has been operating). A year is a good timeframe for promotion and sales forecasting. Within that year, look at your sales by month, holiday, and promotion. Try to get an idea for the next month, the next three months, next quarter, and eventually the next year.

So, what data can be used to forecast?

Data (One to three-year window):

- Overhead
- Purchasing
- Advertising budget
- Average length of time before a prospect becomes a customer
- Length of time between customer buys
- Percentage of customers that buys each of your products

Patterns to Look for:

Popular and Unpopular Products

If you have 10 products, chances are the Pareto principle is at play (80 percent of your customers buy the top 20 percent of your products). If you pay attention to the data, you'll start to see which products are purchased the most by the majority of your repeat customers.

Let's say you promote product A the most, but when you look at the numbers, 47 percent of your customers buy product B and 32 percent buy product C, but only 19 percent buy product A. You can then demote product A and figure out how to promote products B and C to new customers sooner.

If you have a product that not many people buy, ask yourself if it's being marketed correctly, if at all. If it's being marketed properly, the product may be seasonal or not a good match for the market.

Bad Seasons

Heavy seasonal businesses may make 80 percent of their income in a three-month window. Businesses that focus on Christmas pretty much have a 60-day season for their business; they can still get sales year-round via creative discounting, but the vast majority of people don't buy Christmas decorations until they start thinking about Christmas.

Here's the thing: *you don't have to accept the ebb and flow of your business.* You can dictate it by being creative and proactive.

Let's say that every June for the last three years, a company has seen a 30 percent drop on average. Once they know about the dip, they can take steps in to alleviate it, such as creating a special promotion, series of promotions, or finding a completely new product to fill in the gap. If that gap shrinks to 15 percent, that company has just solved a big problem.

Buying Frequency

If you are aware of your customers' buying patterns, you can put them in your forecast and attempt to manipulate them to your advantage. For example, what if repeat customers typically buy three to four products within the first month or two? Right after that first sale, you should encourage them to come back and place another order. You can show your customers retargeting ads, send them nurturing emails, and/or put them into campaigns as quickly as possible to get them to buy more.

Inventory Forecasting

This is all about your products—which products are selling well and which are not selling well, and how quickly products are moving (coming in vs. going out). Even your supply chain plays into this: how long does it take to produce a product? How many days of inventory do you need, and how long does it take to get more?

An inventory is not just the sum cost of the inventory. Inventory takes up space, and space costs money, whether it's in your warehouse or a third-party fulfillment warehouse. Inventory forecasting is critical if you're in the consumable product business because if your products have expiration dates, it's an even bigger issue.

An Approach to Forecasting Inventory:

Step 1: Break it down. How many days of inventory do you have left based on your average sales? For example, if you have

300 items in stock and you fill 10 a day, then you only have 30 days of inventory.

Step 2: Combine your sales and basket forecast, then look at your inventory and see how quickly the product is moving. What are the optimum stock levels for each product when accounting for your supply chain? You don't want to run out, but you also don't want to wind up with too much inventory.

Companies spend millions of dollars trying to get this whole "just-in-time" inventory down. Multinational corporations do it right, but small businesses like us don't have this kind of budget and it's easy to screw it up.

For example, right now I have about $40,000 worth of excess inventory for my kitchen brand. I bought a bunch of inventory because the Chinese New Year was coming up, and when Chinese New Year happens, everybody in China stops working. The port shuts down, nothing gets shipped, and there are backlogs when people go back to work.

I put in extra orders ahead of time, thinking I did the math right (I didn't) and that I needed a bump to get through the Chinese New Year. Now I've got $40,000 of excess inventory on top of what I should have! Will it sell eventually? Yes, but there's $40,000 I can't touch right now. That money could've bankrupted a smaller business, which is why inventory forecasting is critical.

Channel Analysis

Channel analysis involves dissecting how sales are being distributed or acquired through your different sales channels. These sales channels can include Facebook ads, AdWords, or YouTube. The can involve regular ads or something more unconventional, like a YouTube video of yours that happens to refer lots of sales.

Looking at these channels helps you fine-tune your budget allocation. Unless you're a massive organization, your company can only do so much. You have to be tactical and make strategic decisions about what you're doing, and channel analysis is one of the best ways to do that.

We start out at the main sales channel level: organic search engine ads, email drops, your email list, things like that. Most companies only have two or three sales channels, plus maybe some trickle sales that come in from a pin on Pinterest they made two and a half years ago. Usually there's one main core sales channel that drives most of the traffic and a couple of secondary ones.

Things to Look for:

Advertising Budget

If you have three sales channels, chances are a third of your sales don't come from each channel. It's more than likely that one sales channel is driving a large part of the sales.

What about your advertising budget? Is it broken up equally across all three sales channels, despite the fact that one channel drives more sales? If that's the case (and it probably is), you might want to reallocate your budget and spend more money in the most lucrative channel.

Overspending on Customer Acquisition

You may find that you're putting a lot of money in a channel, but your customer cost of acquisition for that channel is higher than you can afford. If so, you need to adjust that cost of acquisition. You should immediately shut off that budget until you can fix it. In the meantime, allocate that budget to a more cost-effective channel.

You may also find that you're throwing money at a channel that's not performing well. If you make this discovery, you should shut that channel down completely. You're better off focusing on growing the channels that are doing well.

Best-Selling Products

Let's get granular for the next level of analysis and look at our best-selling products. Which sales channel is selling which best-selling product the best?

This is more complex than it seems. Let's say Facebook ads are your biggest source of sales, but 85 percent of the sales of your best-selling product came from YouTube. Then you realize you're advertising 10 different products on YouTube.

What if you focused on that high-converting, best-selling product on YouTube? Instead of a $1,000 YouTube advertising budget spread across 10 products, you could have 80 or 100 percent of that budget tied to the product that you already know is making 85 percent of its sales from YouTube. You could also then look into optimizing or reallocating the Facebook ad budget that's being spent on the same product, but isn't driving near the number of sales you thought it was. You're laser-focusing your advertising in sales channels, and that kind of focus pays off big time.

Device Used for Purchase

Are your customers using computers or smartphones to purchase your products? What if a disproportionate chunk of sales is coming from Android users? You suddenly know to dedicate most or all of your mobile budget to Android.

Customer Analysis

Customer data represents all the people who have purchased your products, including one-time customers, repeat customers, and continuity customers. You already know from Chapter 5 that it's important to take note of what your customers are telling you and to make your business decisions accordingly, and you should use all of this data to optimize your sales process, your site, and your advertising. These are your actual customers, so any data clusters you find are 100 percent accurate. There's no guesswork here.

Repeat Customers, Continuity Buyers, and Whales

Who are your repeat customers? If you have continuity, who are your continuity buyers? You want to identify repeat customers and continuity buyers separately because you may want to target them separately.

Finding these people is as simple as rooting out multiple purchase reports. Some platforms pop this data for you right away, but on other platforms you may have to do some sorting in Excel.

Whenever my businesses create one of these reports, we make a list of whales (the top 1 percent of customers). We have a customer service person periodically reach out to those people just to say, "Hey, is there anything I can help you with? We want to let you know we value your business and because you purchased these things before, we realized that you may like this other product." You're selling to them, but at the same time you're calling to check on them. It's an easy way to add revenue while increase customer loyalty.

Regional Affinity

The next thing to look for is regional affinity (your global or domestic business, depending on whether you sell internationally). My Second Amendment business sells in the U.S. because it has the largest gun market and is the only place the Second Amendment exists. When I exported and sorted my customers, I found that that company has more customers in Texas than in any other states. I also found that less than 5 percent of my customers and none of my whales came from California.

Because of that, the company stopped running ads to California completely and reallocated that budget to better audiences. This change made everything targeted, so there were lots of secondary benefits.

For example, since the company has such a regional affinity in Texas, we use geo-targeted campaigns. Most companies run global campaigns that say things like, "Hey, if you like hunting, check us out." Now my marketing team runs campaigns like, "Hey, Texas deer hunter, check this out," or "Hey, Oklahoma pig hunter, check this out."

Those ads are speaking specifically to that market, and the click-through rates are through the roof. Sales conversions have risen as well. Everything just gets exponentially better when you leverage your data.

Demographics

The next thing to consider is customer demographics. You should save any demographic data that you have (and if you took my advice from Chapter 5, you should have a lot) and search it for data clusters or discrepancies. Sometimes you can even collect size data for clothing from demographics.

Payment Preference

If you offer multiple payment options, look up payment preference in your data. Some companies only have one option, but ideally, you should accept at least credit card and PayPal.

If PayPal is your secondary option, usually it's not the most prevalent button in your checkout process. It could be hidden or made smaller than other options. What if the data shows you that a disproportionate number of your best customers pay with PayPal? If you make the PayPal button more prominent or swap the location, your conversion rate could rise. Anything you can do to make things easier for the customer affects your conversion rate.

Shipping Preference

What does the data say about your customer shipping habits? What kind of shipping does your customers prefer? Do your repeat customers typically go for your free shipping or are they upgrading? Do they primarily choose FedEx or UPS?

As you learned in Chapter 4, you can get discounts for bulk shipping with any given carrier. When you offer numerous shipping options, you build a relationship with FedEx, UPS, and the postal service, which can lead to discounted shipping.

The problem is that all of those discounted rates come with volume requirements, so you have to ship a decent amount in order to get your discounts. Let's say you ship 300 packages a day and 100 packages go through each carrier. Unfortunately, that probably won't hit the volume requirements for any of those carriers.

If most of your customers choose FedEx anyway, you could eliminate some or both of the other options. Narrowing the options creates even more discounts because of the larger volume of shipments. You can then increase your profit margin, pass the discount on to the customer, or do a little of both (like me).

Find Your Low-Hanging Fruit

You can capitalize on low-hanging fruit right away. It's anything that's easy to grab and make money off of. Whether it's profiling your buyer's list, building custom audiences on Facebook, or uncovering and taking advantage of honeypot traffic, these fast-action tips can increase hits and conversions right away.

Profile Your Buyer's List

As you've already learned from Chapter 5, the better you know your customer, the better your business is. Marketing decisions, forecasting, targeting–everything is easier. And the more factual the data is, the better.

If you've exported and mined your customer data, you're on the way to making some big statistical discoveries that you can immediately use to improve your business. There are two ways to do this, and I recommend that you use both of them.

Facebook Audience Insights

You might remember Facebook Audience Insights from Chapter 5. Like many of the other demographic tools, you have to enter customer emails or phone numbers to use it (you should do both). Facebook has so much data now that by uploading this information, you can discover a wealth of knowledge.

In addition to all that super-specific demographic data we discussed earlier, Facebook Audience Insights displays usage times and devices used on Facebook, as well as their purchase behavior. How frequently and how much do they purchase? Facebook knows, and you can use that information to tweak your advertising habits.

TowerData

TowerData is an incredibly powerful source of information, especially when you are looking for specific details about your customers. With TowerData, you might be looking for data on whether your customers are interested in a specific subject, but while you're looking for that you may find other statistically significant clusters of interests in your target market.

Not sure what I mean? One of my businesses has a list of over a million buyers who bought a specific type of kitchen appliance. The business has these customers' emails, addresses, phone numbers, everything. My team uploaded this data to TowerData and found three different interests for this group that could easily become three new businesses. We also found that we could use the same customer list to jump-start these new businesses, which all came out of the TowerData research reports. We would've never gotten into those spaces if we didn't already have that data, and it made us *a lot* of money.

TowerData can be expensive, but the cost varies based on the data points you select. If you have a ton of customers, uploading tens of thousands of customers' information might break the bank. To keep the bill down, I extract only my best customers and run just their data because those are the customers I want to learn the most out about.

This is a great service for Amazon sellers to leverage because on Amazon, you're allowed to download a customer's name, phone number, and address, but not their email. In this case, I would upload all of the Amazon customers' information to TowerData in order to extract email addresses (it's well worth the expense). After that, you can put those addresses into an autoresponder to market to your customers via email as well as direct mail.

Curated Facebook Audiences

If you're struggling with targeting, creating audiences on Facebook will be your new favorite activity. Facebook's Custom Audience and Lookalike Audience tools do the heavy lifting of trying to match up the target for you. Whether you're creating segmented audiences of your existing prospects or creating new audiences based on your best customers, these tools set you up for success.

Facebook Custom Audiences

Facebook Custom audiences are made of the people whose email addresses or phone numbers you upload to Facebook. You can segment these people and then target them with specific marketing like retargeting ads, advertising campaigns, or list-building campaigns.

Let's say you have a list of people who've joined your prospect list. They're not customers, but they've opted in for a coupon or a free report. You could create a custom audience of these people and drive ads to a discounted product offer to convert them into customers.

Here's another example: let's say you wanted to offer a lifetime upgrade to your continuity customers for a $100 fee. If you send out the offer via email, not everybody will see it. But if you do it on email, through a custom audience on Facebook, and through a display campaign that shows up on a network of other websites, you've just pumped up the effectiveness of your marketing campaign. While this is happening, you could have another set of ads running to all your other customers. You could exclude your continuity customers from seeing that so they aren't bombarded with multiple offers.

Facebook Custom Audiences also makes laser-targeted campaigns possible. You could make an ad for customers that purchased a specific product saying, "Thanks for buying this product, now check out this." You should leverage your customers because *they are the most profitable group you'll ever run paid traffic to*. They are the most targeted, and the most likely to buy again from you. They'll have the highest ROI of any advertising source you'll ever use.

Additionally, you can use Facebook Custom Audiences to reactivate customers who haven't purchased in a long time. My companies create custom audiences of these customers and run a campaign saying, "Hey, we miss you. Come back, we'll give you a discount." By doing this, we have been able to reactivate as much as 10% of our lapsed customers.

You can create as many custom audiences as you want, and you should consistently update the custom audiences you create. When uploading prospect information, keep in mind that customer emails and phone numbers match up at a much higher rate than prospect emails. Prospects tend to give you a fake email or infrequently used address just to get a coupon or for a free report.

Possible Facebook Custom Audiences

- Opt-In Prospects
- Continuity Customers
- Customers who bought a specific product
- Inactive Customers

Facebook Lookalike Audiences

Lookalike audiences are spinoffs of your custom audiences. Facebook Lookalike Audience analyzes the people in your custom audience and finds other similar Facebook users. It's Facebook's best guess of an audience that's as close as possible to your custom audience.

Did you grasp how great that is? If you use Lookalike Audience on a custom audience of your best customers, *you can create a lookalike audience of other Facebook users who are similar to your best customers.*

This is powerful stuff. You're leveraging Facebook's algorithms and big data collection to help your company find its best customers. Facebook has crazy-smart employees who set up algorithms that crunch the numbers and figure out who this audience should be. Typically, these lookalike audiences are the second most profitable traffic source you'll ever have behind the custom audiences. It's definitely low-hanging fruit.

You can create all kinds of lookalike audiences, and you can adjust how similar the lookalike audience is to your custom audience as well. The more lax you make the criteria, the bigger the audience is. The more focused you make it, the smaller the audience is. You can also add variation and adjust your criteria by degrees.

Facebook Pixel

Anybody who uses Facebook for advertising has a Facebook master pixel, which is a piece of code that goes on every page of the website that you're tracking. When you have this pixel on your website, Facebook tracks anyone who lands on it.

Facebook can also use that data to create a lookalike audience based off website visitors. When you do this, Facebook creates an audience for you based on everybody who has ever visited your website. You can also let this lookalike audience grow on its own based on specific conversions you set up with your pixel. You could create a lookalike audience for people who have added products to cart, purchased specific products, viewed a specific page of your website, or initiated the checkout, but didn't complete the checkout.

Honeypot Traffic

In business, it's not always natural to fully utilize multiple profit centers because you may have blind spots. Honeypot traffic is all about finding the underutilized or ignored traffic sources in your blind spot and bringing them to life. It's about finding that easy-peasy sweet spot, whether it be traffic or unmet opportunities.

What if you found out that a huge chunk of sales for one of your products was coming from a YouTube video? You would focus on more YouTube videos and drive them to that product. This is a chance to leverage the assets you have, and the suggestions in this section are just a few of the options available.

Referral Traffic

If you're getting a lot of referral traffic from a niche website, you could milk it and get even *more* traffic from that site. This is a traffic source that refers sales to you organically. They may not actively advertise your product, but maybe someone mentioned you on the site.

Instead of being satisfied with the trickle of traffic, try to turn it into a stream. Go to that site and see if you can buy direct advertising from them. Can you buy an email drop? Can you buy a banner? Banner advertising is super cheap and works well. It may not have a 6 percent click-through rate, but if it drives sales and makes revenue, who cares?

Most sites have never even been approached for advertising and will be flattered by your offer. If they don't want to sell you space on their page, they may be open to an affiliate relationship with you.

Data-Driven Promotions

Another way to easily increase revenue is to use your data to create specific promotions for specific customer segments or times of the year. If you noticed that two particular products of yours sell well every January, for instance, create a promotion that emphasizes those products every January.

What if you have specific customer segments that tend to buy products within specific price points? Use the price points to create a targeted promotion for that segment of your customers. Let's say you sell car accessories and all these people have purchased steering wheel covers, seat covers, and floor mats. If you have a cup holder liner that's a natural fit for these customers, you could make a promotion just for those people that says, "Because you bought these products, we have a special offer for you on our cup holder liner."

Conclusion

Every ecommerce business has a treasure trove of internal data right under their nose, but few actually take advantage of it. To make the most of this valuable resource, you have to seek out commonalities, patterns, outliers, and gaps in your data and take absolute advantage of them. Doing this may also reveal low-hanging fruit that you can easily pluck to generate more income. Ultimately, analyzing your data correctly helps to improve sales and deliver a better customer experience, and what business owner doesn't want that?

Chapter 7 Summary

Pull all your business data using your ecommerce platform. Use basket analysis, sales forecasting, inventory forecasting, channel analysis, and customer analysis to fully explore and exploit this data.

Find your low-hanging fruit by profiling your buyer's list, using Facebook's Custom and Lookalike Audience features, and taking advantage of honeypot traffic from sources like referrals and data-driven promotions.

PART III

• •

EVOLVED
MARKETING

Part I of this book gave you the foundation for a killer ecommerce business. Part II gave the data you need to capitalize on your market.

Part III will show you how to run the *whole thing*. It's like the fuel that makes everything happen.

You've probably noticed from this book that ecommerce business owners are usually focused on only a few things, and they often forget to pay attention to what's really important. I always say that most ecommerce stores throw crap at a wall and hope something sticks. Large or small, ecommerce enterprises are largely behind the times–they don't know what allows them to stay competitive and maintain growth.

In my time coaching and working with thousands of students, I've learned that most ecommerce business owners often spend lots of time and money on making their website awesome, developing their product, and creating flashy packaging, but they expend NO effort, time, or money on their marketing. When they do think about marketing, they only focus on acquisition. They leave a ton of money on the table, making their lives way, WAY harder.

The reality is that marketing is NOT all about customer acquisition (although that's an important part of it). Marketing also includes prospect acquisition, indoctrination, repeat purchase monetization, not to mention sharing your brand, mission, and company goals with the world. It's an all-inclusive, all-important piece of a business, and you're about to learn how to use it properly.

CHAPTER 8

ADVERTISING CHANNELS

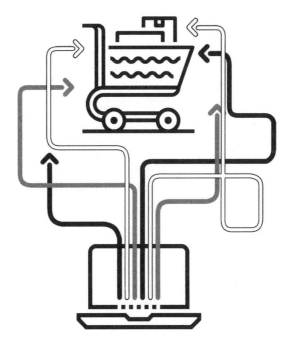

I've found that most ecommerce businesses get marketing channel tunnel vision. They usually have one channel that they started with, or get most of their traffic from, and they become SO focused on it that they don't even consider other channels.

Consider this: if your profitable business only has one marketing channel, opening up *another* marketing channel could double or triple the size of your business almost overnight.

Before we go any further, I need to define what "marketing channel" means to me. A marketing channel acts as an avenue for putting advertising or marketing campaigns in front of your target audience. This is different from what you may find in your college textbook about marketing, which generally only refers to radio, T.V., and mass marketing channels. I ONLY focus (and you should only focus) on direct customer acquisition channels that put specific, targeted marketing in front of your exact target audience.

So, why do multiple channels have such a huge effect on sales? First, they help with perception. The more places you show up, the more professional, relevant, and legitimate you look. If you do it right, there's no way to determine online whether you're a massive company or a 20-something working out of your mom's basement.

Adding another marketing channel is also the fastest way to double the size of your company because when you focus on one channel, you only ever can reach a certain percentage of your market. People are creatures of habit; they inhabit the same circles of the internet, and they rarely stray out of their self-defined channels of media consumption. Some people only use Bing, and other people (like me) never, ever use Bing unless they have to.

The point is, the more channels you have, the broader your reach to that target audience. You'll never reach the entire audience, but each channel gives you access to more people. That's why ideally, your brands and products should be strongly represented in at least four distinct channels.

That doesn't mean that you just jump into four channels immediately—you have to take the time to grow into them. Optimize one channel, get it working, and get benchmark metrics that you can use for the next channel. Keep going, one channel at a time, until you wind up with at least four.

Core Ecommerce Marketing Channels

There are lots of different types of channels out there. Think of your sources as water—many little streams make a big river. It's the same with traffic. Multiple traffic streams, all bringing customers and traffic and prospects and visitors into your marketing, result in a much bigger river of sales.

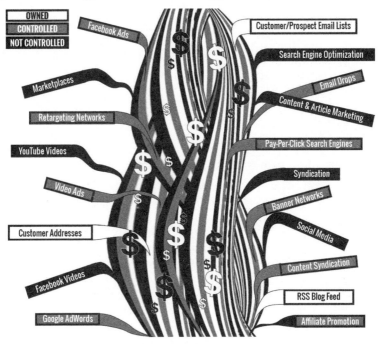

There are more global, broad channels for big companies, but I'm no Coca-Cola and neither are you. We need direct ROI in our advertising and marketing efforts so we can reinvest in our businesses and keep them growing.

All of the marketing channels fall into three broader types of traffic: traffic you own, traffic you control, and traffic you don't control. As you're about to learn, these three types of traffic are not created equal.

Traffic You Own

This is by far the best traffic out there. The goal is to own as much of the traffic as you can because the ROI on traffic you own is *the highest you will ever have*. It's the most on-demand, and it's usually free or cheap to use.

Traffic you own includes your customer and prospect email lists, customer addresses and your Really Simple Syndication (RSS) blog feed (a blog feed that people subscribe to). Owned traffic can be largely automated for ongoing sales, nurturing and ascension, and repeat purchases. You can decide to target your lists with emails, RSS blog feeds, and ads whenever you feel like it, immediately generating traffic and money. You can also send direct mail campaigns to your existing customer base for special promotions.

Traffic You Own
- Email lists (customer and prospect)
- Snail mail lists (customer and prospect)
- RSS blog feed

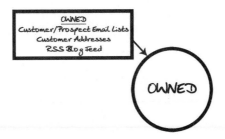

Traffic You Control

This is where 90 percent of your prospect and customer acquisition happens. No matter what people say, the bulk of your traffic generation and customer acquisition efforts should be spent here.

Traffic you control requires active management, time, effort, and capital investment. This is *not* set-and-forget, but it can be accessed when you need it, so you can use paid traffic to grow and scale your business.

Like I said before, the goal is to own all of your traffic. You want to convert traffic you control into traffic you own, which means turning a visitor into a subscriber or a buyer. If you develop a laser-targeted advertising campaign for that person, the next time you market to them they'll be on your email list and the cost of marketing to them will be dramatically reduced.

Within this channel, there are a whole lot of different types of traffic sources, including Facebook Ads, Google AdWords, pay-per-click ads, search ads, and banner ads. Here are some of the most common examples you should be using.

Paid Advertisement

Paid advertisement is the *most important marketing channel* because you can get access to it whenever you need it, and there's no availability limit. The only limiting factor for paid advertising is your budget. It's available on-demand and with infinite scale possibilities.

The fastest way to get your business up and running, or continuously growing and thriving, is to use paid advertisements (as long as you can operate profitably). You don't have to wait for traffic to come in; you can go out and get traffic whenever you want.

The easiest paid traffic source to start with is Facebook. While some other networks have large entry barriers due to cost requirements, Facebook doesn't require a big budget and there's no minimum spending requirement. You can start with any budget you want. If you want to spend a dollar, you can spend a dollar. If you want to spend a hundred dollars, that works too.

Affiliates

Affiliates are a little different than other kinds of paid traffic because you only pay affiliates when they make a sale. Finding good affiliates can be tough, but it can become one of your best traffic sources for customer acquisition once you have all your ducks in a row.

In an affiliate program, affiliates send you traffic and you don't have to pay for any visitors who don't buy; you only pay when the sale happens. You are buying customers, but you are getting direct traffic for free until they buy. You can then retarget those people back to other offers or even to get them to join your list.

Paid Traffic Sources

- **Facebook Ads**
- **Retargeting Networks:** PerfectAudience, AdRoll, SiteScout, etc.
- **Video ads:** YouTube, Facebook, etc.
- **Google AdWords**
- **Email drops**: Buying a placement, such as an ad in someone's email newsletter or physical newsletter.
- **Pay-per-click search engines**
- **Banner networks**
- **Content syndication**: Paying to have your content syndicated across a network
- **Affiliate promotion**

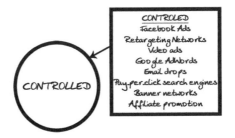

Traffic You Don't Control

There's no shortage of ways to generate organic traffic on the internet. There's always something new: new platforms, new social networks, and new opportunities constantly evolving out of existing networks.

Platform-specific subscriber lists (YouTube, Periscope, Blab, etc.) fall under this category. Even though these audiences are on a platform you can access–they are in your accounts on those platforms, which you can control–you cannot directly control who (if any) of your fans or subscribers will see your message when you post it. Platform-specific subscriber lists are riskier than other types of traffic because if the platform shuts it down, you lose the list. While you have access to the list, though, you might as well use it, as these lists can be a great way to get your message out to your audiences in an engaging and easy-to-consume format.

Even so, traffic you don't control is the most frustrating type of traffic. It comes in when it feels like it, and you have no control over how it comes in. It can't be counted on, but when it does come in, you're very appreciative that it did.

Most ecommerce e-tailers perceive traffic they don't control as free traffic, and that's where most novice e-tailers focus the majority of their efforts. But as Principle 6 says, there's no such thing as free traffic! There's always a cost, so creating traffic takes more effort than buying traffic and should be looked at as a long-term game plan. Here are some of the best ways to create traffic for your business that can then be converted into owned traffic.

Marketplaces

We already discussed the importance of leveraging multiple markets. Making your products available in more places can increase sales, cash flow, and brand awareness for your business. This includes all the marketplaces where you can sell your product–Amazon, your ecommerce store, eBay, wherever.

Why is this a good idea? Some buyers shop predominantly on eBay; others shop predominantly on Amazon (Amazon's target market is basically everyone). If people go to your store and they don't buy, well, maybe they'll buy from you on Amazon because they trust Amazon and they still want your product. Other folks would rather shop at your store. You can give all of these customers *exactly* what they want just by selling in multiple marketplaces. And once you make that sale (wherever it comes from), you have converted that customer's information into owned traffic.

Keep in mind that not all of your products have to show up in all of your channels. In my Second Amendment brand, I think we have a little over thirty Stock Keeping Units (SKUs) right now on our ecommerce store. Only four of the thirty products are on Amazon.

Why is that? Well, each product has its own costs, profit margins, weights, and sizes, and each of these variables interacts differently on different platforms. Take Amazon, for example. They charge a fee for every product you sell that usually works out to somewhere around 20 percent, which might eat up too much of your profit on a particular product.

Similarly, some platforms have too many other sellers offering similar products, which can drive your product price down. If you stay on your own channel, you can sell at a higher price.

In short, types of buyers—and the acquisition cost of those buyers—varies by channel, so some of your products may be better left out of a particular channel. It all depends on the product, market, and channel.

Organic or Unpaid Advertisement

Organic and unpaid advertisement is all about SEO. Organic traffic includes SEO traffic from Google, Bing, and other traditional search engines, but it also includes YouTube videos, blogging, content marketing, article marketing, and syndication.

This traffic is indirect–you can optimize for it and do everything you can to encourage it, but it's ultimately not up to you whether any of it works. For example, when you write articles or guest posts or when you use content syndication (promoting your content on other sites), you don't have any control over the quality or quantity of the traffic.

Social Media

We already talked about paid traffic on Facebook, but the social media side of Facebook–fan pages and groups–is completely different. Social media marketing channels includes all social networks, such as Pinterest, Instagram, and Twitter.

You can have a following on social networks, but ultimately you have limited control over who sees what you post. The reach is dictated by algorithms that you don't control, as well as by the audience itself. You also can't control the traffic that comes in because it's dictated by the responsiveness of the users.

Comparison Shopping Engine (CSE)

Customers want to see what's available, so when they need a product, many of them search for the product on Google. Google runs Google Shopping, the largest CSE in the world. There's another similar search engine called TheFind.com that's also popular.

CSEs drive traffic straight from the search results to your site. If prospective customers find your product in a comparison shopping engine and they click on it, it takes them to that product listing page on your site.

Google Shopping and TheFind.com are free product comparison shopping engines; just upload your data and your product feeds and they'll display in search results when customers search for that type of product. There's also a whole subset of paid comparison shopping engines that require either a flat fee or charge a pay-per-result or pay-per-click fee to include your products in results. Shopping.com, Shopzilla, and NexTag are all examples of paid CSEs.

Comparison engines are popular because they can steadily refer sales. They probably won't be your biggest channel, but they are low maintenance (you don't have to do anything once it's set up) and they get your products in front of a subset of your target audience that you might otherwise have missed.

Unpaid Traffic Sources

- **Search engine optimization**: Optimize your content, site, and product pages to rank as high as possible on various search engines.

- **Social media marketing**: Actively promote your product across various social networks (posting on your Facebook pages, tweeting, pinning stuff to Pinterest, Googling, etc.)

- **Content marketing**: Blogging and guest posting. Your posts must then be optimized so they can generate more traffic for you.

- **Video marketing**: This has become the way of the future online. It includes posting videos on YouTube and uploading videos to Facebook.

- **Press release distribution**: Draw up a press release and distribute it to various networks–the media could pick it up and then drive traffic to you. Additionally, this could bring you even more publicity if a media source sees your press release and likes your product.

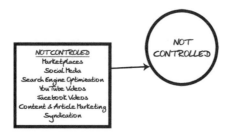

Tips for Channel Success

Now that you know about the different channels, I want to tell you how you can use them to the fullest. I've seen too many business owners make these mistakes, sometimes at the expense of their whole company. Read this section carefully so you'll know exactly what to do (and what not to do) to grow your business through multiple channels.

Avoid Channel Dependence

While you can use all these channels to maximize your product's selling potential, you absolutely *should not* become marketing-channel dependent.

It's easy, especially online, to become dependent upon whatever channel is driving the majority of your traffic or bringing you the most sales. Tunnel vision naturally sets in. But while it's important to try to squeeze the maximum value in conversions and sales out of your most lucrative channel, depending on only one channel can hurt you.

Channels can dry up or change their rules. If you are dependent on a channel that dies, you're in trouble. That's happened to me before.

In my hunting business, some of our gun accessories were on Google AdWords, and they were doing very well. Things changed when Google became "anti gun" overnight. Suddenly, we were no longer able to use AdWords to market our product and we had an immediate 40 percent decrease in sales. We had been too heavily dependent on that AdWords channel, and had we been a weaker business with no other strong marketing channels, we likely would've folded.

It's also important to avoid dependence because channels rely heavily on users, and users have a tendency to evolve. Just look at Myspace! Myspace would've been considered a top channel from 2005 to 2008. Now it's been completely transformed into a music promotional platform with less than one tenth of the traffic. It's not that the site changed; users just moved on.

I know of many businesses that were too dependent on Myspace. Once Myspace dried up, the businesses did too. You don't want to be that business owner.

Always remember that one of the keys to surviving change in the marketplace is branding (remember Principle 8?). Branding crosses all channels. If you're branding, it doesn't matter if Facebook shrivels. People still know your brand, and your customers would just go find it somewhere else. You're not just selling them a widget that's unattached to a brand; you're selling them a product *within* a brand.

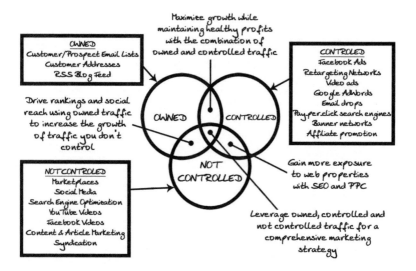

Take it Slow

There are a whole bunch of ways to generate traffic–the important thing is that you don't try to use them all and that you don't try to use them all at once. Just like with anything, you have a finite amount of time. The more things you try to focus on, the less gets done and the less progress you make.

Master one traffic source at a time. Don't move on until you can be *sure* that the channel is maximizing your sales and generating tremendous traffic.

Breach Consumer Ecosystems

I've already mentioned that people typically use the exact same sources to consume media, so you only reach a certain percentage of your market if you only advertise in small areas or subsets of your market.

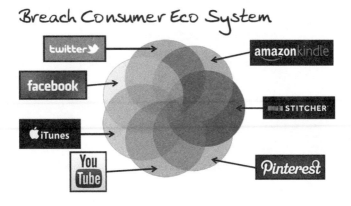

Breach Consumer Eco System

On the other hand, some audiences as a whole reject specific *types* of media channels.

If that's the case in your market, then you should avoid those channels. If your market is elderly people who are not very tech savvy, you might discover that YouTube is not the right channel for you to use. If your audience is huge on Facebook and lousy on Twitter, then Twitter should be at the bottom of your list and Facebook at the top of your list. You can push Twitter to the side until you've leveraged all the other bigger and better traffic sources.

To do this, you have to *know your demographic*. Research how your target audience interacts with each type of media source, rank them in order of usage, and react appropriately.

Traffic Temperature

An ecommerce relationship is no different than a real relationship between two people. Just like you wouldn't ask someone you just met to marry you, you shouldn't try to push a sale on a brand-new visitor. You have to nurture the relationship first–you have to educate, deliver value, and foster trust before asking for the sale.

The amount of nurturing you have to do for your customer depends on the temperature of your traffic. I sort the different types of traffic coming in using cold, warm, and hot temperature classifications. The colder the traffic, the more abundant it is; the warmer the traffic, the rarer it is and the more likely it is to result in sales. These temperatures dictate your marketing process for that type of traffic, whether you push them to become a customer immediately or later down the road.

Cold Traffic

What It Is: These are people who have never heard of your business before.

Communication Method: The communication method for cold traffic is paid traffic and organic traffic. The vast majority of paid and active marketing efforts goes toward connecting with cold traffic. This is the largest pool of traffic available to your business.

Goals:

1. **Get them on a retargeting list** so you can show them more of your content. If they're browsing your website, you need to track their activity. Let's say they look at dog collars and dog beds. If you track them, you'll know that they are interested in those products and you can show them retargeting ads. You're trying to increase the likelihood of converting them from prospects to customers.

2. **Convert them to an email prospect**. Get them to give you their email address in exchange for a coupon or some kind of freebie.

3. **Indoctrinate them**. Tell them who you are and why they should be a customer of yours.

Warm Traffic

What It Is: These are people who are somewhat familiar with you but have not purchased yet. They are on your prospect email list and your retargeting lists. They can also be Facebook fans, Twitter followers, or YouTube subscribers.

Communication Method: Retargeting ads, email marketing, and direct offer ads through paid networks.

Goals:

1. Convert them to an email prospect, if they're not already.

2. Convert them to a customer. Get that initial sale.

Hot Traffic

What It Is: These are people who know you well and have purchased from you at least once.

Communication Method: Retargeting, email marketing, and direct mail. Most of your advertising efforts should be focused on cold and warm traffic. Your hot traffic marketing will be largely taken care of with automated campaigns.

Goals:

1. **Increase the frequency of purchases**. They've already bought from you at least once–now make it a regular occurrence.

2. **Increase the average order size** in order to increase the amount of money they spend each time they purchase.

It's important to remember to use different language and tone as you communicate to each of these different types of traffic. While you're building your marketing campaign, ask yourself: what's the temperature of the people who see this campaign? Use information about your traffic to tailor the messages for your customers, then focus that campaign to fit that specific type of traffic.

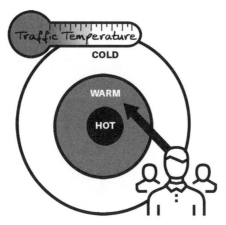

Conclusion

Not everybody is the same, and so not all of your channels should be the same. The more channels you use, the more people you will attract, period. Plenty of business owners forget this, but now you have the key to growing your customer base.

If you're new to adding channels, I would choose one to start with and go from there. I always encourage my clients to start with whichever channel fits their existing strengths or talents. If that doesn't work, then my default is Facebook paid ads. Not all traffic sources have to be like fire hoses–if one traffic source doesn't generate as many sales as another source, you shouldn't automatically label it as a bad. Just keep at it, strengthen each one as you go, and watch the customers pour in. Remember, many streams make a river.

Chapter 8 Summary

There are three types of traffic: traffic you own, traffic you control, and traffic you don't control. Traffic you own includes your prospect and customer lists; traffic you control includes paid traffic; and traffic you don't control includes organic and social media traffic.

Slowly build up the number of marketing channels you use until you have a diverse group of channels. Remember not to become overly dependent on a single channel.

Use your knowledge of cold, warm, and hot traffic to turn prospective customers into repeat buyers and to increase sales and brand and company awareness within your customer pool.

CHAPTER 9

FRONT-END MARKETING

The front end is the flashy gateway into your business. You demonstrate the value of your communication, content, and products here as visitors get to know your brand. It's where you build the initial relationship with your prospects and customers, and that's why most ecommerce businesses only pay attention to front end marketing.

Despite all that focus and flash, when it comes down to it, the front end only has three purposes:

1. Converting traffic into prospects

2. Converting traffic into customers

3. Converting prospects into customers

Did you notice that I didn't mention profit in that list? That's because the focus of the front end of your business is NOT to make a profit.

People get confused about this. The business owners who are busy focusing on front-end marketing usually ignore everything else because they're trying to extract profit from the front end. Doing that actually keeps their business *small* and prevents them from ever achieving any sizable growth (or any sizable profits, for that matter). Although you *can* make money on your front end (and you often will), you shouldn't be making that a priority.

This chapter is about the strategy and foundational marketing elements that help grow ecommerce businesses. It can be applied to any business, no matter what your niche or goal. The rules in this chapter—from improving your front-end conversions to creating and marketing content to leveraging retargeting pixels—will streamline and simplify your business, leading to more revenue, bigger profits, and less stress for you.

Why Traffic Is Not Your Problem

Have you ever heard something along the lines of, "If only you could get more traffic, then you'd make more money"? The reality is you probably don't actually need more traffic to make more money, unless of course you have zero traffic—that's a different problem entirely.

If you have zero traffic, then what I'm about to teach you will not do anything for you until you start generating traffic. But if you *do* have traffic, you probably don't need more of it (yet).

Why? Here are a few depressing stats and figures about traffic:[26]

- 99 percent of site visitors don't buy on the first visit.

- 70 percent of website visitors leave without *ever* checking out anything you have. Of the 30 percent that's left, roughly 84 percent leave after they've looked at a product they were potentially interested in.

- Of the people who view a product, 8.5 percent add it to cart and never check out. 5 percent add the product to the cart, start filling out their payment details, and then abandon the transaction.

- Only about 2.5 percent of the customers who view a product actually complete the purchase.

Why pour more water into a leaking bucket? You're losing a ton of your current traffic because of your bounce rate, product or page abandonment, and shopping cart abandonment. Instead of seeking more traffic, learn how to optimize these areas to start making the most of your existing traffic.

It's easier to sell to an existing customer than a new one, and it's much easier to convert your current traffic than to get

---

[26] 2016. Sap Hybris. Retrieved from https://hybris.com/en/marketing/marketing-convert

more. Fix the leaks, make more money, and worry about getting more traffic once you can handle it.

Combating Your Bounce and Abandonment Rates

Let's talk about your bounce rate–the visitors who immediately leave without even viewing a product first. A lot of factors can affect your bounce rate:

- **Page load time.** Most people have a 12-second attention span or less[27], so if your page loads slowly, that's a big problem. Use Pingdom and Webpagetests.org to find what's slowing down your load time and try to fix it.

- **Page content.** Does your content correspond with what led traffic to your site? If what people see on the site is different from what your ad led them to expect, they will bounce. Also, if your spelling or grammar is off or the site just looks shady and weak, people will bounce.

- **Visual appeal (or lack thereof).** Simple works, but ugly chases away potential buyers. If your page is too busy, with no clear action for a visitor to take, they bounce. Make sure to have a clear path for them to follow.

- **Use Exit Intent Offers.** It's too easy for people to leave most sites. Exit offer pop-ups are a quick fix that says, "Don't leave, check this out instead!"

---

[27] McSpadden, Kevin. "You Now Have a Shorter Attention Span Than a Goldfish." Time. May 14, 2014.
http://time.com/3858309/attention-spans-goldfish/.

Implementing a good exit offer takes around 20 minutes and, in my experience, can give you a 2 percent lift in opt-ins. From those opt-ins, you should see roughly a 10 percent lift in sales.

The same variables that cause a high bounce rate on your landing page can also affect product listing page abandonment. If your listing pages are ugly or uninformative, visitors leave. If the pages don't have a clear call to action or aren't congruent with your visitors' expectations, visitors leave.

But *life* can also happen. You've probably had your online shopping interrupted by a phone call or another distraction before. You can't stop the outside "life" distractions from occurring, but you can try to get people back on the page and to the product afterwards.

Retargeting is one of the best ways to keep the product at the top of someone's mind. I've got a whole section on that for you later in this chapter, so first, let's discuss another important aspect of front-end marketing: *how* you advertise.

Active Advertising

Here's a quote that I live by and also beat into the heads of all my students: "The ability to grow a business and produce income comes down to being able to *use paid traffic to break even or better.*" This sets the stage for active advertising. Remember how I said that paid advertising was so crucial in Chapter 8? Here's where that really comes into play.

Active advertising is buying traffic to generate visitors for your landing pages, funnels, and squeeze pages (a lead generation page that collects email addresses). You can then convert these visitors into prospects and customers. It's all about maximizing acquisition—acquiring as many customers and prospects as you possibly can for every dollar that you spend.

In fact, this is so vital that you should spend **50 percent** of your advertising budget on active front-end advertising. I don't mean your whole marketing budget; I'm specifically referring to your advertising budget (money you've set aside to spend on ads for customer acquisition), which is hopefully substantial.

Focus your active advertising efforts on no more than two traffic sources. As you may recall from the last chapter, if you spread yourself too thin, you can't get anything done. You won't get the results you could from focusing not only your budget, but your attention on just two sources. You could use Facebook ads and Google AdWords, or Facebook ads and Instagram, for instance, but using Facebook ads, Instagram, Pinterest, AND AdWords would be too much unless you have a massive budget and the inventory to support that much traffic and sales.

If you're just starting out and don't have an established business or a large advertising budget, then focus on just one traffic source at first. Get it dialed in and converting, and bringing in an ROI that's worth it. Getting $3 for every dollar you spend is ideal and is what I typically aim for, but try to break even at the very least.

Customer Acquisition

Spend the vast majority of your active advertising budget (70 or 80 percent) on customer acquisition. This is for acquiring new customers by promoting products and funnels that are already selling well.

You're not trying to drive traffic to a brand new product; you're focusing on what converts. Follow the Pareto Principle when determining which products to use for this: which 20 percent of your converting products drive 80 percent of sales? Those are the products you should drive even MORE traffic to.

Prospect Acquisition

Prospect acquisition is the next focus of your active advertising campaign. It's all about getting people to give you their email address so you can convert them to traffic you own and market to them for cheap or free. This should only account for 10 to 20 percent of your active advertising budget; it's an important element, but it's not the main driving force of your active advertising.

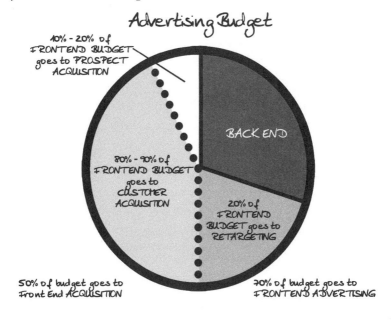

253

A New World of Online Promotion

So, how should you advertise to your target audience? Direct response marketing–driving people straight from the ad to offer–used to be the default answer. It was once the god of marketing, and though it isn't dead yet, it's a dying art form that is becoming less effective and more expensive every day.

Ready for some depressing statistics? In America alone, $170 billion was spent on direct marketing in 2013, with a conversion rate of less than 3 percent.[28] Click-through costs are higher than ever, with a 65 percent increase between 2014 and 2015 alone[29]. Email deliverability and open rates are in the toilet, and Facebook ads increase in price up to 335 percent per quarter[30].

Most importantly, Facebook and Google–the two biggest traffic sources on the internet–don't like advertisers. We're the ones that give them money, but we're not their customer. They don't like or care about us; all they care about is the end user–the consumer.

Consumers are becoming smarter and more tech-savvy about the buying process as well. They're harder to sell to, and direct response tactics just don't work as well anymore. That's why the algorithms have changed and advertisers have more restrictions on how they are able to advertise on the networks.

---

[28] The Economist Print Edition (2013, May 25). No Hiding Place. Retrieved from http://www.economist.com/news/science-and-technology/21578357-plan-assess-peoples-personal-characteristics-their-twitter-streams-no

[29] Hochman, Jonathan. "The Cost of Pay-Per-Click (PPC) Advertising-Trends and Analysis." Hochman Consultants. November 24, 2015. https://www.hochmanconsultants.com/cost-of-ppc-advertising/.

[30] Garner, Patricia. "Why Facebook's Ad Price Rapidly Increased in the Fourth Quarter." Market Realist. February 11, 2015. http://marketrealist.com/2015/02/why-facebooks-ad-price-rapidly-increased-in-the-fourth-quarter/.

If your ad gets reported, it gets shut down right away. When you mess with the user experience—if you use any kind of normal marketing—you have issues. We have to play by the platform's rules, even though those rules are constantly changing and are sometimes even kept secret. We just have to constantly adapt.

Campaigns and Content

Traffic used to be the king, and the offer was queen. Traffic is still king of the game, but there's a new queen in town: content. The offer has been demoted. It's not nearly as important as the content because nowadays without the content, you can't get your traffic to see the offer in the first place.

At the same time, campaign promotion has replaced direct promotion. Instead of traffic going straight to the offer, traffic now goes to a content piece on a site you control first. The content piece drops a retargeting pixel, which then fires a retargeting ad that promotes the offer.

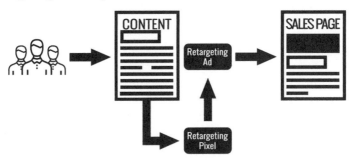

This is the new world of marketing. You advertise the content, and the way the visitor interacts with that content determines whether or not they progress into your funnel.

Retargeting campaigns tie it all together (we'll discuss retargeting in depth later in this chapter).

Content has tons of advantages. It allows visitors to get to know you and your products without the pressure of a sale; it establishes you as an expert and authority in the marketplace; it's dirt cheap. If you've ever run a pay-per-engagement boost to a post on Facebook, you know how inexpensive it can be.

And guess what? You can't constantly run an offer, but you *can* constantly run content. Content always gets approved. No network rejects a nice blog article, native ad, or viral content piece. And if you build up an asset (blog or authority site) with your content, it can, over time become a traffic platform too. You'll start getting organic, natural traffic and your site's content will start ranking for long tail (a string of keywords, like "How do I get six-pack abs?") and product-related keywords in the search engines. It'll become an asset that can be leveraged over and over again, and that content can be constantly remarketed and pushed out. That content will remain effective at driving sales for years to come.

Since content is now every bit as important as the offer, you have to be smart about it. The more viral potential the content has, the better. You can further extend your advertising budget by getting people to share, like, and comment on your content.

Leverage and integrate topics that are trending when possible. You also need to write in a language that your audience speaks; every market has a lingo, a collection of words and slang that are unique to them. If you picked your niche because it's lucrative, but you don't really "get" your audience, you need to learn how they speak because people who identify with a niche don't want to buy from an 'outsider.' If you have a customer avatar, use it to help you write good content that speaks directly to your target market.

Don't create 20 different content pieces that go on 20 different networks; create one amazing piece of content to leverage across multiple networks. Once you have viral-worthy content that speaks to your target market and incorporates mentions of the specific product you are trying to sell (soft sell), repurpose that content across multiple networks. Make your content work *for* you.

How do you double your sales? Broadcast your content marketing campaign on another traffic source! What about five? Let me show four different high-quality traffic sources that were previously unavailable to you in the direct promotion model. Each of these traffic sources work exceptionally well when combined with the content campaign promotion you learned above. Now I'll show you some of the actual results we experienced—case studies, if you will.

Stumble Upon

Have your content piece listed on StumbleUpon so that people can "stumble" on it and share it with other StumbleUpon users. When I used StumbleUpon I got a thousand paid stumbles resulting in over 20,000 page views in 30 days, and it only cost 9.6 cents per thousand views.

Reddit

Reddit is a forum-like content site that now allows paid ads on their site. In one of our recent tests, we got 298 laser targeted clicks for only $0.16 per click. There's not a massive volume of traffic available, but the Reddit user base is hyperactive and typically very passionate about their niche.

Twitter

Twitter ads have been great for my businesses. When I first used it, I got 617 engagements for 65¢ each and 93 front-end conversions. Not the cheapest traffic, but converts very well for selling physical products.

Outbrain

Outbrain connects you with tons of other sites that allow paid content promotion. It works best with viral-type content that serves the bigger niche markets. If you are in a super targeted niche, it might not do well for you (still worth a test though). For me, it generated 48,819 targeted clicks for less than $0.06 per click—that's a *lot* of traffic. The conversions from Outbrain are not as high as those from the other traffic sources mentioned here, but with the volume of traffic available and low cost, I can still make consistent break-even sales on the front end and then turn a profit through the funnel.

Owned Media (Traffic You Own)

Your retargeting and email list, as well as your content, are all owned media. Traffic you own is the best and cheapest kind of traffic to leverage, which is why it surprises me that more businesses don't use owned media to drive massive amounts of highly targeted and high-converting traffic to their content promotion campaigns. If you use your owned media traffic resources in conjunction with paid media, it can amplify your ability to go viral, give you credibility in the marketplace, and blow up your sales.

Retargeting

You've finally made it to the retargeting section I keep talking about! You may remember the definition of retargeting from Chapter 6; it's when a pixel tracks which product in your online store a visitor may be interested in, then triggers retargeting ads that show the person ads for that product as they visit other websites.

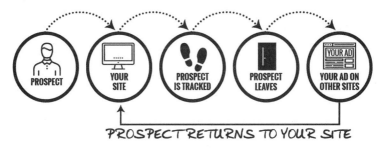

I can't stress enough how important retargeting is. Retargeting accounts for over *40 percent* of my sales in all niches, and it consumes just 20 percent of the advertising budget because it's so cost effective. You'll get almost the same reach (if not more) from retargeting as you'll get from active advertising.

Leveraging Traffic with Retargeting

Retargeting initiates the sales cycle in the content sequence, attracting clicks that take visitors to your various product offerings. It's important to note here that retargeting ads only inspire the *click*, not the sale. Many marketers try to get the ad to do the selling as well as generate the click, which is actually counterproductive to your overall goals. Let the ad get the click, then let your landing page do the selling.

Retargeting is an owned media source, just like an email list. You send an email to your email list and get instant traffic; likewise, you can simply turn on a retargeting campaign to your retargeting lists and get instant traffic. It's an on-demand traffic source you can use at any time. There are two key metrics for retargeting that you need to be aware of:

- **Cost per pixel (CPP)**: Media cost divided by the number of pixels placed. Pixels are worth money, so you need to leverage them as a revenue source, just like you do with your email subscriber list.

- **Value per pixel (VPP)**: Income generated divided by the number of pixels placed. How much money are your pixels making you? Believe it or not, these numbers can be rather large.

Your media budget should be focused on driving traffic to the *content*, not the offer. If you're using a sales funnel, you should send people to your content and use retargeting ads to get them to the sales funnel. Focus your king on your queen.

What does that mean? If you're selling a silicone cupcake mold, for example, you shouldn't make your content piece about that product. Instead, create an article that people who buy silicone cupcake molds would like, such as an article about how to make devil's food cupcakes. Use pictures of your silicone cupcake mold being used to make the devil's food cupcakes and incorporate some soft selling (you could mention that silicone cupcake molds make baking cupcakes much easier), but don't do any heavy or overt selling.

When the user visits your cupcake recipe page, drop a retargeting pixel. Actually, don't just drop one; I usually drop five pixels from five different retargeting networks (it gives me more reach). Once you do that, you can use retargeting ads to show your offer or lead capture page.

Your retargeting campaign then displays ads all over the web saying "You liked the devil's food cupcake recipe? You may like this silicone cupcake mold!" Depending on your business, you may retarget them straight to an offer or take them to an opt-in form to get their email before taking them through the rest of the sales cycle.

You can segment your retargeting list just like an email list, and you can (and should) have multiple retargeting lists. I have hundreds of retargeting lists broken down into segments, sub-segments, niches and categories, buyers and non-buyers, prospects, etc.

When it comes to retargeting as part of your front-end marketing strategy, there are three core retargeting promotions you should run at all times. Once they are set up, all of these core promotions run on autopilot, with very little interaction required from you besides monitoring.

1. Cart Abandonment Promotion

Cart abandonment promotions are for visitors who add a product to their cart, but don't complete the checkout. The fact that they added a product to their cart shows they have a high interest in actually buying it. These are people with the highest likelihood of purchasing that product.

A cart abandonment promotion automatically retargets customers who do this, showing them ads all over the Internet saying, "Hey! Don't forget about this item!" The goal is to bring them back to make the purchase. Often cart abandonment promotions are sequenced with discounts or escalating incentives the longer the item has been in that person's cart.

Cart abandonment promotions are an effective way to recoup sales. They need to be running all the time, and they need to be set up so that they are automatically triggered and ended without any action from you or your staff. The second the customer buys the product or after the time limit you set expires, the system stops retargeting that person. This is automated follow-up marketing at its finest.

2. Specific Product Promotion

Specific product promotions run based on people's viewing habits, not necessarily what they've added to their cart. They showcase individual products that visitors view on your landing pages. If they've viewed a product, this promotion tries to keep that product at the top of the mind by showing the person ads for the product. It can also send them to a video review page that gives them more information (and perhaps a coupon).

Here's another trick: after someone still hasn't purchased a product after going through your retargeting sequence, you can activate a retargeting campaign that sends the person to your Amazon product listing for the same product. Oftentimes the reason the person hasn't purchased from you is because of the lack of trust or comfort with your brand, and giving them the option to buy your product on Amazon eliminates that concern.

3. List-Building Promotion

List-building promotions are for people who visit your site and have been retargeted with specific offer promotions but don't buy anything. Just like prospect acquisition campaigns, they are useful for targeting the prospects in your market who are resistant to buying from somebody they don't yet know, like, or trust.

You can run the same type of promotions you use for your prospect acquisition campaign–a coupon, a lead magnet, or some kind of giveaway–as a way to remarket your potential prospects. This gets these offers in front of people as many times as possible for the lowest possible cost, which is what retargeting is all about.

I prefer to use list-building retargeting campaigns to target general site or blog visitors, as well as anyone who did not convert from another product-specific retargeting campaign. Just because you don't get the sale doesn't mean they won't buy later. Getting them onto your list gives you the chance to build a relationship that will turn that person into a solid customer.

Email Marketing

One of my friends is a famous businessman (who I'd rather not embarrass, so I won't mention his name) with an email list of over 400,000 people. He's a successful guy with multiple best-selling books, but he was going through some financial trouble and he reached out to me for help. When I found out about his gigantic email list, I told him to leverage it and send those people an email selling one of his products.

This businessman was TOTALLY opposed. He had never done that before and he didn't want to start. He promoted his products on Facebook and on his blog and his customers bought them, but he had a mental block against sending emails because he thought his customers would not buy from an email. Ultimately he completely refused to do so, and his business (and income) suffered heavily as a result.

This is not uncommon. Plenty of people have mental blocks about sending emails, but in the ecommerce space, email lists are automatic money in the pocket. You set an email campaign up in your autoresponder and you forget about it–it just runs in the background and continuously converts your prospects into customers. This not only puts money into your pocket, but also moves these new customers into the back end of your business where you can maximize their LTV.

Email Away

Most businesses owners are not marketers; they don't think about email marketing from a marketing mindset, so they don't send nearly enough emails. My aforementioned friend is a great example.

The truth is, the more emails a business sends, the more money it makes. Ideally, ecommerce businesses should email every day or every other day. If you think every day is too much, you're wrong. The more frequently prospects get emails from you, the more they think about you and the more likely they'll be to make a purchase. You aren't a spammer for doing this; it's just effective email marketing.

To automate your email marketing, you have to build email campaigns and plug them into an autoresponder sequence in a linear fashion. The autoresponder sends each one of these emails on a specific date or at a specific time after someone joins your list. The prospect joins your list and gets the first email, and in a day or two they get the next email, and so on for as long as you have emails scheduled.

I like to aim for long autoresponder sequences. Most ecommerce brands, if they even build a sequence, only do so for probably 7 to 14 days long at the longest, and then stop–they never email prospects again. Email marketing is not a primary focus and they don't know what they're doing, so they don't think about it. They know they should send an email and they do so periodically, but that's about it.

Luckily, you know better than that. Your first goal, if this is a new concept to you, is to build out a single 30-day sequence. If you build one that long for the first time using the formula I'm about to give you, I can almost *guarantee* an immediate 10 to 30 percent boost in converting prospects into customers. You would have to screw everything up to not see a sizable lift in sales.

Once you have that 30-day sequence, work on increasing it and adding more emails and promotions. Do this until it's a 6 to 12-month long email sequence.

I know people that have 36 months of emails programmed. I currently have a 16-month sequence for people on my prospect list in my Second Amendment niche, and I get sales like clockwork from people at all stages of that list. Even people who are on day 374 of 480 might decide to buy; you never know when someone will decide to become a customer.

You might have noticed that I'm only discussing email marketing to *prospects* here–people who have joined your email list but have not yet purchased anything from you. The second a prospect or visitor becomes a customer, they're taken off the prospect list and added to a customer list (we'll get to customer email marketing in Chapter 10). Make sure to add an automation rule to remove them from the prospect list the second they become a customer; that way, people only receive prospect emails for as long as they are prospects.

The conversion rate of prospect email marketing varies depending on your business. There's no set standard, and certain markets have much higher rates than other markets. The Internet marketing space, or make-money-online space, has the lowest opens and the lowest click-through rates, whereas a market with grandmothers who crochet may have ridiculously high open and click-through rates because they don't think about it as marketing.

Either way, though, email marketing is worth doing because it absolutely always results in more sales and new customers, which is the primary goal for the front end of your business.

Creating the Content

If you can't write, then you should outsource the job of writing these emails. But if your issues are superficial–punctuation and that kind of thing–then write them yourself and have an editor review them.

Remember, you're writing for the internet, and unless your market research shows that your target audience are sticklers about grammar, it's okay not to scrutinize too hard. Done is better than perfect; you can always go back and revise.

If you need to hire somebody, then hire somebody who knows what they're doing! Don't hire someone who doesn't understand conversion or AIDA (Attention, Interest, Desire, and Action for the customer). You should also try to find somebody who can write in the voice you're looking for, and stick with that person to write the sequence. If you hire a bunch of writers, there may be inconsistencies in the voice throughout the sequence, and you don't want that.

Always Track Your Emails

I always stress to my students that they need to track all emails sent in their email marketing campaigns. Not many businesses do this kind of tracking because it takes work and is not the easiest thing to set up. But if you're spending money on advertising, don't you want to know if it's effective?

You need to track everything you possibly can. The more tracking data you have in place, the better you'll be able to troubleshoot and make things better.

Certain platforms require multiple tools to assimilate all that data for tracking, but there are link tracking or click tracking programs that let you know where your sales come from. ConversionXL, Improvely, and CPV Lab are the three big tracking software companies. I use Improvely because it's easy to use and it has a nice dashboard interface that makes the data simple to understand.

In my businesses we have a tracking link for *every* ad and *every* email that gets sent out. I can see, for instance, that the second email in my core promotion campaign has made 57 sales and the seventh email in that same campaign has made four sales but generated 842 clicks (which tells me there is a problem). You have to be specific so that you can optimize your business for maximum results

If you set up link tracking, you'll know if the sixth email you sent out is not getting opened. That could mean that the subject line is not appealing to your prospects, so you can edit the subject line and see if the open rate increases.

Everything can be improved and made more effective, but ONLY if you have the data to tell you what is and isn't working.

Dealing with Unsubscribes

Every time you send an email, even if you're giving away your best products for free or offering crazy discounts, you'll to get unsubscribes. This happens every time you send an email, so you might as well stop worrying about it. Besides, what's the point of having a list of 30,000 people who you don't email just because you're afraid of someone unsubscribing?

I personally mix it up so it doesn't get boring, but I don't let more than two days go by without sending out an email, EVER. Sometimes it's every day, sometimes it's every other day.

I mix it up a little bit so there's not a pattern. You don't want your prospects to notice a pattern or they'll start to glaze over whenever they see your email. But if you're doing everything right, making money, and still having people unsubscribe, just know that that's normal. You're not doing anything wrong and you should keep sending emails.

Types of Email Campaigns

There are three core types of campaigns for prospects: the indoctrination campaign (beginning), the core offer campaign (middle), and the bucket campaign (end). These campaigns are essentially a series of emails for prospects.

Types of Email Campaigns

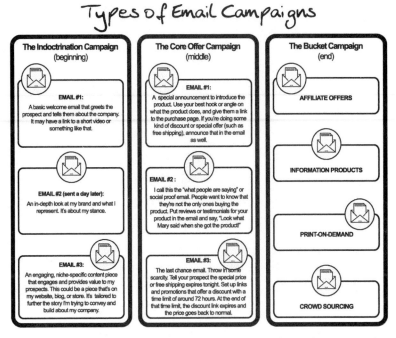

The Indoctrination Campaign (beginning)	The Core Offer Campaign (middle)	The Bucket Campaign (end)
EMAIL #1: A basic welcome email that greets the prospect and tells them about the company. It may have a link to a short video or something like that.	**EMAIL #1:** A special announcement to introduce the product. Use your best hook or angle on what the product does, and give them a link to the purchase page. If you're doing some kind of discount or special offer (such as free shipping), announce that in the email as well.	**AFFILIATE OFFERS**
EMAIL #2 (sent a day later): An in-depth look at my brand and what I represent. It's about my stance.	**EMAIL #2 :** I call this the "what people are saying" or social proof email. People want to know that they're not the only ones buying the product. Put reviews or testimonials for your product in the email and say, "Look what Mary said when she got the product!"	**INFORMATION PRODUCTS**
EMAIL #3: An engaging, niche-specific content piece that engages and provides value to my prospects. This could be a piece that's on my website, blog, or store. It's tailored to further the story I'm trying to convey and build about my company.	**EMAIL #3:** The last chance email. Throw in some scarcity. Tell your prospect the special price or free shipping expires tonight. Set up links and promotions that offer a discount with a time limit of around 72 hours. At the end of that time limit, the discount link expires and the price goes back to normal.	**PRINT-ON-DEMAND**
		CROWD SOURCING

When people join my prospect list, first they get the indoctrination email campaign, which is composed of three emails. After that, they move into my core offers promotions and get the first, second, and third core promotion emails for my best-selling product. If they still haven't made a purchase, then I'll send the first, second, and third core promotion emails for my second best-selling product.

You never stop sending prospect emails until someone unsubscribes from your list or finally buys a product. Once that happens, the person moves to a customer email list, but until then you have to keep sending them prospect emails.

The Indoctrination Campaign

This is the first email campaign prospects receives after subscribing, and it starts with a welcome email. These people barely know you or your company, and the point of the indoctrination campaign is to start the process that will get them to know, like, and trust you enough to become a customer. They may have seen your ads a couple of times, but they don't have a good relationship with you yet; they haven't even agreed to purchase one of your cheapest products. In terms of traffic temperature, they are lukewarm at best.

The goal is to introduce your business and tell your prospects who you are and what you stand for. You're indoctrinating them into the who, what, and why of your brand. Why are you different? What can they expect from you? They need to be told what to do.

These emails should be full of the voice and personality you want to convey. Don't try to sell them anything; instead, make them comfortable and start to build trust.

Another advantage of the indoctrination campaign is that it trains prospects to click on your emails. Always include links in all of your emails to train your buyers or prospects to click on them. If you never include links and then suddenly include them, they probably won't click them, but if you always have links, they'll get used to clicking. Without clicks there will be no sales.

Specifics

An indoctrination campaign could be one email or several; it depends on personal taste and how much the first email explains. I do a three-part indoctrination campaign that's written conversationally, in a voice that appeals to whatever market I'm targeting. You're more than welcome to do something similar. Here's a quick breakdown:

Email 1: A basic welcome email that greets the prospect and tells them about the company. It may have a link to a short video or something like that.

Email 2 (sent a day later): An in-depth look at my brand and what I represent, including the names of any charities or special interest projects we support.

Email 3 (one day after): An engaging, niche-specific content piece that engages and provides value to my prospects. This could be a content piece that's on my website, blog, or store. It's content that's tailored to further the story I'm trying to tell about my company.

The Welcome Email

Everybody gets tons of emails that they delete without opening, but one email that the vast majority of people open is that welcome email. In fact, in my experience it has *four times* the open rate of other promotional emails and *five times* the click-through rate. Welcome emails can also see more than *three times the transaction and revenue per email* as compared to regular promotional emails.

Go ahead and read that again. Yes, the numbers are staggering. Your welcome email is valuable real estate, and you're probably not doing anything with it aside from introducing yourself to people.

How can you take advantage of this opportunity? One of the easiest ways is by including a simple coupon. Offer free shipping for orders over a certain amount, or offer 10 percent off their next order. It doesn't have to be anything crazy—just a simple coupon will suffice. It's a way to show the prospect that you appreciate them.

Make this offer casual, not a heavy pitch (remember, that's not the purpose of the welcome email). My businesses have gotten as high as 12 percent take rate on that coupon. Even if a prospect doesn't take advantage of it, they still remember that you offered it to them, and that helps them trust you as they move on with your marketing sequence.

In addition to including an offer, be sure to give some thought to the content of the welcome email. The companies that have good engagement and build big followings are the ones with engaging storyline-type emails that customers look forward to reading. If you're curious about this, I have an email marketing course that teaches people exactly how to write this kind of content–see the products section of BuildGrowScale.com for more details.

The Core Offer Campaign

Core offer campaigns sell and convert prospects into customers. These are emails designed to promote and sell your core or best-converting products.

Since this is the first attempt to sell, it's important to keep the barrier low. Remember, they've just gone through your indoctrination and they're still in that lukewarm phase.

Usually, the core offers you promote to your prospect list are the exact same ones that are in your active advertising campaign. Use tripwires, flash sales, loss leaders, and other similar tactics to give people a chance to buy and test your product, customer service, and order process without investing a large amount of money.

Specifics

Each of the core products promoted during the core offer campaigns should get its own email campaign sent over a period of three to six days, either everyday or every other day. I've found that a multipart email campaign, consisting of at least three emails, generates *four to five times* more sales than a single email. It's definitely worth the effort.

I usually break each product campaign into three parts. You could send four or five emails, but I started noticing diminishing returns after the third email in a campaign, so I just stick to three.

These are the three types of emails I use in a core promotion sequence. Create these three emails and try to vary them up a little bit. You should make a sequence for every single product you promote with your autoresponders to maximize your returns.

Email 1: A special announcement to introduce the product. Use your best hook or angle on what the product does for the prospect and give them a link to the purchase page. If you're doing some kind of discount or special offer (such as free shipping), announce that in this email as well.

Email 2: I call this the "what people are saying" or social proof email. People want to know that they're not the only ones buying the product, so put reviews or testimonials for your product in the email and say, "Look what Mary said when she got the product!"

Email 3: The last chance email. Throw in some scarcity. Tell your prospect that the special price or free shipping expires tonight, you're running out of stock, or whatever type of scarcity you are using. When I do a promotion, I offer the discount with a time limit of around 72 hours. At the end of that time limit, the discount link expires and the price goes back to normal. When I send an email to a prospect and say, "Hey! This offer expires in 72 hours!" It does exactly that for that specific prospect. A prospect who gets the same promotion tomorrow also get a 72-hour window.

Tips for Featuring Different Products in Your Core Offer Campaign

 Start with your best-selling product first, put your second best-selling product next, and so on.

 Mix it up so you have a variety of different price points and types of offers in your campaigns. Vary the price points; don't make all of them 20 percent discounts, and don't always do free shipping offers or flash sales.

 Keep adding more product promotions to your autoresponder (you never know what people will bite on). The autoresponder will get longer and longer as you continuously expand it.

 You can recycle a core campaign and use it again in three months or six months.

 Some businesses do ridiculous last-chance promotions. If you use scarcity in your promotion, make sure you do it right; you want it to enhance sales and boost conversions. If people realize that you're using *false* scarcity, they won't believe you anymore. I don't believe in using false scarcity at all. Yes, I use scarcity all the time, but I don't lie about it. You're trying to build a relationship, and if you start with lies, how will you build a good one?

Bucket Promotions

Bucket promotions are additional promotions or miscellaneous offers that you can run through your prospect list. When you send a bucket promotion, you're just trying to mix things up to extract some extra money out of that lead. I send these after I've sent all of my core offers, but you can also mix them in between your core promotions to space out offers to your own products.

I learned about bucket promotions from Ryan Deiss and Perry Belcher, rockstar marketers and owners of DigitalMarketer.com and Native Commerce, a long time ago. They asked me why I wasn't doing it, and I told them that it was because I wanted to promote my own stuff. They explained that I was leaving a ton of money on the table from a list that's not buying from me, and as long as they are on my list, I might as well try to get some money from them even if they don't want my products. The first year I added bucket promotions to one of my businesses, I made an extra $100,000 in sales.

As you can see, bucket sales can add up, and the bigger your list, the more you can make. As long as the prospect stays on your list, you need to keep trying to sell them something, whether it's yours or someone else's. Bucket promotions can make you an easy extra income.

Once I've hit a prospect with all of my offers without converting, at that point they're the least valuable lead I have, but there's still a chance that they could buy something. This is when I send them affiliate offers, information products, or print-on-demand items (I don't have to inventory them, and I just get a commission when they sell). Let's say you are leveraging a platform like Canvus for t-shirts and Gearbubble to do mugs and jewelry that relate to your market; those are value add-ons that many of your prospects would probably be interested in.

Remember, though, that whenever you do an affiliate promotion, you are in effect giving somebody else your customer in exchange for money. You're giving away the customer. On this prospect list, the initial goal should be to acquire the customer yourself.

If a prospect buys something you promote as an affiliate, even though you make money, they still stay on your prospect list; they don't get bumped to your customer list. Bucket promotions are totally acceptable for boosting your income, but don't rob your business by putting someone else's third-party promotion ahead of your own offers.

Default Promotion Vault

Most ecommerce businesses struggle to figure out what promotions to run next. They try to come up with promotions when their revenues are down or at the last minute instead of planning ahead.

I've been there. It can be hard to come up with ideas for different promotions on a continual basis, but at the same time those continual promotions are critical to a businesses' success. To combat this problem, I've created what I call a default **promotion vault** for my businesses.

A promotion vault is a collection of default promotions that run at least once a month during specific times of the year. These are promotions that I use every single year, starting with New Year's Day promotions on January 1st. I promote these via ads and emails to both customers and prospects.

This simple promotion vault strategy guarantees that you have at least one active, scheduled promotion each month. Some months lend themselves to more than one promotion easily, so you can have multiple default promotions for some months. In November for example, you have Thanksgiving, Black Friday, and Cyber Monday.

However, you don't want to have tons of default promotions; one every five days would be overkill because it doesn't allow you to have any kind of flexibility. If something new comes up, you can't promote it because you have all these default promotions blocked out on the calendar. But you do want to have at least one per month, and up to three per month can be very effective if you have no other promotions that need to go out.

When used correctly, the promotion vault helps to stabilize your business' monthly cash flow. You'll be able to count on a more regular cash flow each and every month based on these promotions, which allows you to forecast more effectively and plan for both business growth and inventory purchasing.

But the default promotion is not just for revenue; it helps with all aspects of your business, including your mental health. There is nothing more stressful than an empty promo calendar. If you plan this out in advance and you leverage some default promotions, your calendar doesn't look nearly as scary. In fact, it could actually make you smile.

The default promotion vault is one of the biggest time and stress relievers that I've put into my businesses, and it's one of the things that my customers and consulting clients thank me for teaching them after the fact.

Types of Default Promotions

There are five main types of default promotions that you should have in your vault—I have all of them in mine. Let's go over the basic types of promotion here.

1. Holiday-Based Promotions

Holiday-based promotions can be for Christmas, News Year's Day, Valentine's Day, Mother's Day, Father's Day, Halloween, Easter, St. Patrick's Day, Memorial Day, Labor Day, President's Day, you name it. They are the easiest because usually there's at least one holiday every month of the year. Many traditional holidays already have links to specific merchandise–President's Day is big for cars and furniture, for example–but all the other holidays can lend themselves to almost every business. Even a mountain biking store can have a Valentine's Day promotion if it's tailored to the market. You may not want to capitalize on every single holiday, but at least there are plenty for you to choose from.

2. Commercial Date Promotions

Commercial date promotions include Black Friday, Cyber Monday, Super Bowl, and Back to School. They are commercially-created shopping dates, and they can be very lucrative for your business because your customers are already looking to spend on these dates.

3. Brand-Related Promotions

These promotions tie into your brand. The one that all brands can pull off is the anniversary promotion (for the anniversary of your company and store). A lot of companies make a big deal out of this; in the brick-and-mortar world, a store can offer free food, music, and other amenities. You can do something similar online–make a big hype about it and offer a huge blowout promotion with special incentives only seen during your anniversary sale.

4. Charity or Cause Promotion

Charity or cause promotions can be generic; you may want to do a promotion tied to World Cancer Day and donate a percentage of your profits to a cancer foundation, even if your company has no obvious connection to cancer research. But promotions that focus on charities with a direct connection to your brand or market work the best. For instance, brands that sell children's products could create promotions that benefit charities that help children, such as the Make-A-Wish Foundation.

5. Niche-specific Commemorative Day Promotions

Nowadays, there's a day for almost anything. There's an International Yoga Day, World Sleep Day, Geek Pride Day, and so on. Before social media, you probably would never have heard about World Sleep Day, but now you might see it on your Facebook feed. If you sell anything related to sleep, this is a good day to capitalize on. If not, just find a list of all the internationally accepted commemorative days and look for one that fits your niche. If you sell to a specific demographic area, find commemorative days that are unique to that state, county, province or country and create a promotion around them.

Building Your Promotional Calendar

I hope that gave you some ideas on promotions you could use to help you fill out your year. Write them down, map out the entire year, and create a calendar for these promotions. Once you have at least one default promotion for every month of the year, fill in your additional product-specific flash sale, or other promotions that you've already decided to do for the year as well.

Once you add everything up, you should have three promotions mapped out for each month of the year. For a 30-day month, you should have a promotion every ten days. Space them out and get some time in between them.

You should build complete promotional campaigns for each of these default promotions. For example, each promotion needs a themed landing page. Figure out your product specials and discounts. Will you bundle products? What are the special offers for this promotion? Get the graphics, ads, and emails done, then create a folder for each of these campaigns and their source files.

You might have noticed that I always stress keeping track of the numbers, and promotional campaigns are no exception. Each year you run the campaign, make sure to keep track of all the stats. Record everything that happened, and what was good and bad.

The next year, with a little editing and tweaking, you can relaunch the same campaign and it should perform better. Aside from improving the campaigns, all you have to do is basic annual editing. Change some dates, maybe change some of the products, but by and large the campaigns are plug-and-play.

Even if you had to scramble two days before a promotional holiday, at least 80 to 90 percent of your work is already done. While your competitors panic and pull all-nighters to get campaigns running, you can kick back and relax.

Conclusion

Too many of the business owners I meet try to use the front end to generate a profit. As you now know, the front end is really all about *acquisition*. Your goal is to turn traffic into prospects, traffic into customers, or prospects into customers.

If you can focus on those three things, you'll let the front end do what it does best. And of course, when you let your front end do its job, in the end you'll make more profit than all your competitors who are trying so hard to squeeze out both a profit and a customer on the front end. You'll outsmart the market–and reap the benefits in a big way.

Chapter 9 Summary

Traffic is not your problem (unless you have zero traffic). There are many factors that can lead to high bounce and abandonment rates. Fix those problems to unlock the true potential of your current traffic.

Spend 50 percent of your advertising budget on active front-end advertising. 70 to 80 percent of that budget goes to customer acquisition, while the remaining 20 to 30 percent goes to prospect acquisition.

Direct promotion is dead, and while traffic is still king, content is the new queen. Drive traffic using primarily content campaign marketing.

Retargeting is currently the best way to get cheap traffic. You can make massive ROI when you couple retargeting with good content.

Don't be afraid of email marketing because it can almost guarantee an immediate 10 to 30 percent boost in converting prospects into customers. Don't forget to track all emails you send through your email marketing campaigns (if you're spending money on advertising, don't you want to know if it's effective?).

CHAPTER 10

BACK-END MARKETING

Chapter 9 was about the front end of your business, where you acquire customers and prospects. That's the part that everyone likes to think about, but it's less than half the battle. The back end is what separates the pretenders from the winners

The back end is not about acquiring more customers. Instead, it's all about customer retention and maximizing the

LTV of customers you already have. Here, the goal is to retain customers and maximize the profit you get from them.

Back-end marketing is heavily neglected in most ecommerce businesses, so this is the first area I inspect when I work with a new client. Many business owners are so focused on that front-end acquisition that they don't pay much (if any) attention to the back end. To make matters worse, lots of business owners don't know what to do on the back end to make more money, besides maybe sending an occasional email.

I'm excited about this chapter because back-end marketing is powerful–super powerful. It can double or triple the revenue and profits of your company with only a marginal increase in expenses, all without any new customers. And it can do it in a matter of MONTHS, not years.

This is one of the main reasons that my ecommerce brands are so successful. There are many competing brands that acquire more customers than I do, but my back end is so dialed in that I make more money with fewer customers than they ever could. The back end can be heavily automated, so the vast majority of what makes my companies run happens automatically.

How does all this work? Well, you already know that I like the Pareto Principle–In any ecommerce business, 20 percent of customers drive 80 percent of the future revenue. Therefore, the focus of back-end marketing is to maximize that top 20 percent.

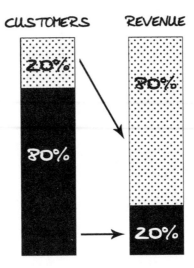

There are two ways to maximize your top 20 percent: keep them around longer and buying more frequently, or turn a regular customer into one of those top customers.

These strategies are all about customer retention, but the magic is that it does double duty in building up the back end of your business. First, it increases the retention and money earned from existing customers. At the same time, it increases the retention and income potential from future customers who will continue to come in the door from your front-end marketing.

Every customer goes through this back-end sequence, so when you set your back end into place, its profitability exponentially grows as you acquire more customers. Simple tweaks to the back end make an immediate impact in the bottom line, and they also set the stage for larger profits later as all the new customers come in.

I'll start by outlining a few important things to look for within your ecommerce business that will allow you to make the most of your back-end ecommerce operations. Back-end marketing incorporates a lot of tactics from previous chapters (especially Chapters 7 and 9), so you'll get to use what you've already learned to improve how you do things on the back end.

Customer Life Cycle

Everyone is aware of product, business, and industry life cycles. Customers have life cycles too. As Jim Novo, the author of *Drilling Down*, says, "Customers are always in the process of changing their behavior–either accelerating their relationship with you or terminating their relationship with you."[31]

Just like knowing that the temperature of your traffic lets you tailor your marketing, understanding the four phases of the customer life cycle allows you to tailor your marketing to the particular phase a customer is in. The more effectively you communicate with customers at each stage of the life cycle, the longer your customers will remain happy and satisfied customers and the more money they will spend with your company.

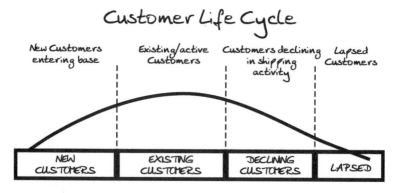

[31] Novo, Jim. (2001). Making Money With the Customer Lifecycle: Trip Wire Marketing. *The Drilling Down Project.* Retreived from http://www.jimnovo.com/Behavioral-Marketing.htm

The Four Phases Of A Customer's Life Cycle

New Customer: This is the first phase. New customers make their initial purchase and begin their life cycle. On the graph, you can see that the line starts to climb in the new customer phase; this is showing the rising potential value of your customer.

Existing or Active Customer: Existing and active customers are in the growth curve; the customer is starting to purchase more. They peak during the active customer phase and eventually reach the peak lifetime value of your average customer. You should strive to keep customers in the active customer phase as long as possible.

Declining Customer: The customer's potential value falls during this phase. People have stopped purchasing as frequently, and this trend will continue to decline. Ideally, you'll catch them at this point and try to bump them back up into the active phase.

Lapsed Customer: Lapsed customers are basically dead customers. They no longer purchase from you, and they are basically dead weight on your customer list. Most companies do nothing with these lapsed customers and simply write them off, but in my mind this is lost potential revenue. The goal here is to try to bring some of these lapsed customers back from the dead. I call this reactivation, and if done correctly, it has the potential to take a lapsed customer and restart their whole life cycle, putting them right back into the prime active customer phase. This alone adds a few hundred thousand dollars a year in extra revenue to my brands.

You can determine the ranges for each customer phase in your business using the data you extracted in Chapter 7. To do this, you need to implement a data search and sorting function. Some platforms can do this internally, or it can be done in excel. Find your constraints and averages for each of the customer types listed above, filter your customer list by those constraints, then sort them into the appropriate customer categories so you can chart them accurately.

Granular Segmentation

Granular segmentation is one of the main elements of effective back-end marketing. If you don't start doing it correctly and actively when you first build out your back end, the rest of your back-end marketing efforts won't work well.

For me, segmentation means separating people into groups based on specific criteria. Granular segmentation involves getting VERY specific about criteria and sorting customers into various lists.

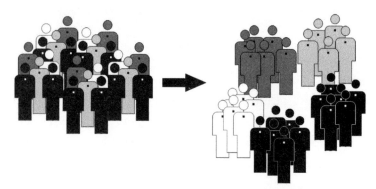

You already learned that sorting your customers into different categories allows you to target them individually and lets you send out multiple promotions to different segments simultaneously. Instead of everybody getting that same promotion at the same time, different groups can receive specific customized promotions offers based on what you know about them.

In my businesses, granular segmentation of our customers has boosted my return on back-end ad spending by **1,200 percent** for active advertising and retargeting. No, that isn't a typo.

Email can be just as dramatic. In the ecommerce industry, an email customer list without segmentation is generally considered to be worth roughly 20 cents per subscriber. If you email a list of a thousand people twice a week, that's 20 grand worth of income over the course of the year.

But it doesn't have to end there. In fact, it shouldn't because 20 cents per subscriber is TERRIBLE. Please don't ever be satisfied with that. A friend of mine, Drew Sanocki, does a lot of private equity-backed ecommerce consulting, and with properly segmented and targeted back-end marketing campaigns he's seen list value numbers as high as $9 per subscriber. That's a **5,000 percent increase** in revenue thanks to segmentation, and that is only for email. Imagine what you could do with active advertising and retargeting.

If you want to experience some of those massive increases for yourself, there are a variety of different categories into which you can segment your customers:

- Products bought and browsed

- Category of products within your business that they are interested in

- Customer location and demographic

- Amount of money spent

- Repeat customers or whales (the top 1 percent of customers in your business). Whales spend *30 times more* than other customers in my businesses, so they're a very important group to target.

There are four main places in the back end where granular segmentation works:

Inside the Ecommerce Store: This is the deepest level of segmentation possible, as your ecommerce platform stores all the key sales and customer data. Using this data, you can easily create segments based on customer life cycle stage, products purchased, total spent, and most frequent repeat purchasers. You can also create segments for the top 1 percent, 5 percent, 10 percent, and 20 percent of your customers, and those are just a few of the different and profitable segments you can create from your ecommerce data.

Email Autoresponder: Inside an email autoresponder, you can set up different segmentation based on the products that customers purchase. Some email autoresponders create separate lists while others create tags that are assigned to the profile, but either way, it's all based on past purchases. When a customer buys a product, they're added to a list or tagged for that specific product; they buy the next product and it happens again. This is specific email segmentation that can be mirrored in your advertising or retargeting network segmentation.

Active Advertising Sources: Like you learned in the last chapter, active advertising builds audiences through targeting and code snippets that track conversions on your sites. Active advertising sources include Facebook, Google AdWords, Pinterest, Bing Ads, and the like, and it's possible to create segmented lists of your customers and prospects based on their actions in each of these advertising sources. You can then run advertising campaigns to each of those lists independently or in combination with other customer segment categories.

Retargeting Platforms: Use those same platforms as we talked about in Chapter 9 here. Just like with active advertising sources, you can set up different segmented lists (for example, a different list for each product purchased or a list of everyone who viewed a specific article on your blog). Set up segmenting on all the different platforms that you use so that if you wanted to turn on a campaign that targeted everybody who purchased product A, you could do just that and exclude everyone else. If you didn't have that segmentation in place across all these different platforms, the impact of your advertising would shrink significantly.

Back-End Active Advertising

Did you notice that we only used up 70 percent of your advertising budget in Chapter 9? That leaves us with a total of 30 percent to use on the back end of your business. 15 percent of your advertising budget goes to back-end active advertising.

Front-end active advertising targets only potential customers, so back-end active advertising only targets that relatively small, specific audience of existing customers. It could be a few hundred to tens of thousands of people, but it's still significantly smaller than the audiences you market to on the front end.

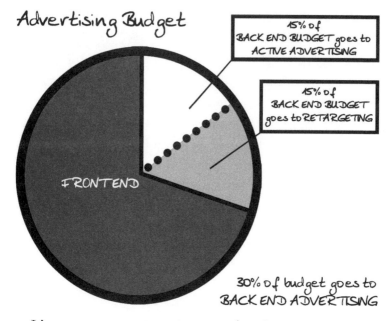

Advertising Budget

15% of BACK END BUDGET goes to ACTIVE ADVERTISING

15% of BACK END BUDGET goes to RETARGETING

FRONTEND

30% of budget goes to BACK END ADVERTISING

It's easy to want to target more than just your customers on the back end, but you should not give into that desire if you want to build a successful business. The back end involves laser-targeted and micro-segmented advertising focused on the hottest owned traffic in your business. That's why the ROI is exponentially higher on the back end than it is on the front end.

Back-end active advertising targets the four segmented lists I just mentioned (store, email list, active advertising sources, and retargeting). Just like in your front-end marketing, you should focus your efforts on no more than two active traffic sources (Facebook and Google, for example). If you're only using one source, use the same source for both your front and back end. If you're using two active traffic sources for your front-end, use those same two for your back-end. Otherwise, you are breaking Principle 5 and you may end up stretching yourself too thin.

Repeat Purchases: The Focus of Back-End Active Advertising

Back-end active advertising is all about *repeat purchases*. These customers have already purchased at least once, and the point of running these ads and buying this media is to get them to buy again and again.

You no longer need to promote your loss leaders or trip wire products to your existing customers. They have already made the decision to become a customer, gone through your indoctrination campaign, and are now at a level of comfort and awareness that allows for the promotion of your regular margin offers. When you have a sale or special promotion, then by all means alert your customers. But by and large, do not run your existing customers through acquisition sales funnels.

If you took Chapter 2 to heart and focused on building a recurring income core, your first goal is to get existing customers to join the continuity program. If that is your focus, then by all means use trip wires or loss leaders to get your customers in front of your continuity program with the best chance of converting the sale.

Aside from promoting your continuity program, you can use back-end active advertising to show your customers offers that may interest them based on their previous purchasing habits and segmentation. This gives you the highest likelihood of generating repeat purchases.

One word of caution: don't market something a customer has already purchased to that customer unless the product is consumable. If it's consumable, by all means market it to them again because they'll run out and they've got to buy it again. But if it's not consumable, find the most tightly-related product to the one they already purchased and pitch them that.

Back-End Retargeting Promotions

The remaining 15 percent of your total advertising budget should be spent on back-end remarketing and retargeting promotions. Use all of the networks that you learned about in Chapter 9 (such as PerfectAudience, AdRoll, and SiteScout) to build these segmented customer audiences. Remember to set the email lists and networks to automatically exclude any prospect or visitors, since back-end retargeting is only for customers.

You want to implement back-end retargeting pixels as soon as you can so they can collect data and start building your various retargeting lists, even if you're not using that network to run retargeting ads at the time. It doesn't cost anything to simply plant the pixels and code, and if you decide to use the network later, you already have HUGE customer lists built and ready to utilize.

Core Retargeting Promotions for Existing Customers

There are three core promotions I use to retarget customers on the back end.

1. Dynamic Product Ads

Dynamic product ads are an advanced form of retargeting that automatically shows customers products based on their previous purchasing habits. Rather than displaying a random product, dynamic product ads use data to show the most *relevant* products. This is platform-specific and 100 percent automated.

There are apps that, depending on what ecom platform you use, plug into your store and create feeds for dynamic product ads. The apps plug into Facebook, Google, and other platforms and take it from there. They use auto logic as the basic setting, but it's always better to figure out your own logic in the advanced settings to match up with the customer data you already have.

2. Customer Reactivation

Customer reactivation campaigns target customers at the tail end of their customer life cycle with your business. Many of these customers may already have completely lapsed and gone dormant, and the focus of this campaign is to get them back.

How can you do that? Try to get them to make another purchase. Attempt to revive dead customers with crazy good deals, discounts, or special offers. Only a small percentage of them will take the offer, no matter how good it is. But as you learned in a previous chapter, a 5 percent increase in customer retention can lead to a 25 to *95 percent increase in profits.*

Customer reactivation promotions are automated campaigns that can be triggered in two ways. First, they can be activated based on a time limit; if a purchase hasn't been made or a pixel hasn't fired in X number of days, the campaign starts automatically.

More commonly, the customer reactivation campaign is tied to a segmented email marketing campaign. The store sends an HTML email marketing campaign with retargeting code in it to declining and dead customers, and if that email is opened, it triggers the customer reactivation marketing campaign. I'll go into much greater detail on this topic when we cover the Win Back Email Campaign later in this chapter.

3. Active Advertising Support

Active advertising support campaigns are short-lived retargeting ads that run alongside any active advertising campaign you have running to your customers. If you are doing a promotion for a specific product to your existing customer base, you should always include a retargeting campaign to help boost the campaign's effectiveness.

This is a more manual process because you have to set up every campaign for each promotion, whereas dynamic product ads and customer reactivation campaigns are completely automatic. Even so, they are worth the effort because they boost the efficiency of ALL customer advertising campaigns by as much as 30 percent. The support campaigns start as soon as your active advertising promotion begins and ends when the promotion ends.

Email Marketing on the Back End

In Chapter 9, you learned about active (broadcast) email marketing for promotions and campaigns. But that's not the case that with the back end. Here, email marketing means targeting existing customers with automated email promotions sent by an autoresponder. These automated back-end campaigns are the closest thing to being able to print money out of thin air that you will ever find. You set them up once and they spit out sales each and every day thereafter.

Four Types of Campaigns

There are a huge variety of campaigns ecommerce businesses can use for back-end email marketing, but there are four main campaigns that every ecom brand needs to incorporate. All four of these campaigns are triggered by customer behavior and segments.

1. New Customer Campaign

During the new customer campaign, your job is to welcome the customer to the family and create that sense of belonging. These customers have just paid, you're shipping them a product, and you want them to keep buying from you. You have to build a relationship and a rapport with them.

Typically, the new customer campaign is three to four emails in length depending on how you want to space information out. Whether you send one email or four, there are a few ways to make this campaign successful.

In the new customer campaign, the customer welcome phase could be a couple of emails long. There are two key points to a new customer welcome campaign:

- Remind them who you are, what you stand for, and what your mission is. Building loyalty starts with that sense of belonging, and that sense of belonging helps with the repeat purchases.

- Make them feel like they are part of something special, like they *belong*. Bring them into the story of your company, then provide value to them with niche-specific content. For example, if you sell cooking accessories, you could send them recipes, exclusive chef interviews, or product reviews. Show them that you are interactive, enthusiastic, and more than just an online store.

2. Targeted Offer Campaigns

Targeted offer campaigns involve getting your buyers to buy something else, turning them into repeat buyers. This is one of the most important campaigns you can run, and just like your core offer campaigns on the front end, these can be scheduled and automated.

Targeted offer campaigns are your default promotions featuring best-selling products. They might be higher-priced point offers (not necessarily tied to discounts) because existing customers don't need constant special prices or incentives to buy again.

Customer segments come into play with targeted offer campaigns. People who bought product A get targeted offers that relate to product A; if product D is not related, that customer won't receive an offer for product D immediately. The more segmented and targeted these campaigns are, the more successful they will be.

Since targeted offers are based on customer segments, at any one time you may have many different campaigns going out to different segments. Each campaign targets smaller audiences than a generic promotion, but they're more tightly focused and better targeted—and they have higher conversions as a result. But keep in mind that as more and more of your customers become repeat customers, they will start to show up on multiple different segmented lists. Therefore, it is very important to set up some rules and structure in your targeted offer campaigns to prevent one of your best customers from getting bombarded with multiple targeted offer campaigns at the same time.

3. VIP Campaigns.

VIP campaigns are targeted specifically at big spenders. These are the whales, that top 1 to 5 percent of customers that buy all the time without much incentive.

The aim with VIP campaigns is to build loyalty so they keep buying. Make these people feel special, but think *rewards*, not discounts.

These people already buy. You can give them an occasional special deal, but they're buying a lot already. They don't need to be incentivized with discounts; they already love you and like to buy from you, so think of other ways to keep them engaged and feeling special. There are lots of ways to do this:

- Give them perks, like loyalty points and upgrades on their shipping

- Send them special gifts such as a mug or company t-shirt

- Develop a special access 1-800 VIP number for them to call in and get their own rep to take their orders.

- Set up VIP status tiers with increasing levels of perks based on spending.

I want to elaborate on that last one with a good example. I shop a lot at Banana Republic, and every time my level of spending increases, they give me a higher level of elite status. For example, at my current level I get free tailoring with rush turnaround on anything that I buy. There are also special shopping days on their online store where elite members can access certain items first. Both of these perks have a low cost to the store, but provide cool value to me and encourage me to spend even more.

I highly recommend the 'elite member' tactic. Set up different levels of VIP status based on the amount spent. Each time a customer ascends to the next level of spending, kick off another automated VIP campaign. If someone exceeds your highest level, make a new level.

You could publicize your VIP program, but you don't have to. It just happens automatically to make your VIP customers feel special. If they don't know that it'll happen, they feel even *more* special. They're more likely not only to continue to buy from your company, but also to openly praise your company to their friends and on social media. Rewards programs do a fantastic job of turning your best customers into product evangelists and brand ambassadors.

4. Win-Back Campaign

Each day a certain subset of your customers are nearing the end of their life cycle with your company. They're not excited about what you're offering any more, they had a bad experience, or maybe they're just moving on. The win-back campaign brings dormant customers back to life or gets customers who have stopped purchasing often to start buying more frequently again.

Defection Times

To execute these win-back campaigns, you have to use the customer data that you learned how to exploit back in Chapter 7 to determine your average defection time. Statistically, the longer a customer goes without purchasing, the less likely they are to purchase again. Usually, if a customer goes a certain number of days without purchasing, they don't purchase again. This is called your Average Defection Time (ADT). For most online stores, that's between 30 and 50 days (it varies based on the market).

Measure your defection time using the data you mined and use it to schedule out and structure your win back campaigns. If your defection time is an average of 30 days, trigger a win back campaign to start at 31 days.

Techniques for Winning Back Customers

One of the best tactics for trying to revive a dead customer is to "give away the farm." Come up with a crazy offer–the bigger and the more unbeatable the offer, the better.

The reality is that only a small percentage of lapsed customers even bite on the offer. These people are already on their way out, so any percentage of them that you can get to come back can make a big difference. Statistically, the number of people who take action is so small that you can *afford* to give away the farm.

A good win-back campaign can either fully or partially reset the life cycle for that customer. In my business, these win-back campaigns alone generate about $300,000 a year. This is additional revenue that comes in on autopilot–once I set the campaign up, I just sit there and watched the money roll in.

One of the more effective methods I use to enhance the win back campaign is the tiered ladder promotion. I create a ladder-style promotion based on my defect rate, and it escalates the size or impressiveness of the offer in tiers based on the length of time that the customer hadn't purchased. For example, if a customer has gone 30 days without purchasing, the tiered ladder promotion could trigger a win-back campaign that looks like this:

- 30 days no purchase: 15 percent off their next order

- 45 days no purchase: 25 percent off their next order

- 60 days no purchase: 35 percent off their next order

- 90 days no purchase: 60 percent off their next order

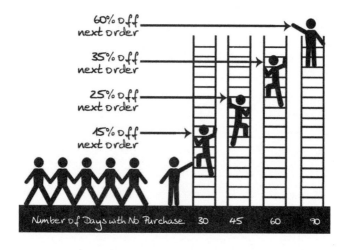

If at any point during this ladder promotion the customer takes the offer and makes a purchase, the win back campaign automatically ends. At this point you have just brought a customer back from the dead and have a chance to reset their customer life cycle, so you should create a special 'nurture' email campaign to let them know how much they were missed and how much you value them as a customer.

Invest in Your Campaigns

Building these campaigns is a lot of work, so don't try to build every campaign at once. Build the new customer campaign, followed by the VIP campaign, then the win-back campaign. Once all the campaigns are active, add new layers to each one.

Just like I said in Chapter 9, set up tracking for all your campaigns. Track email open rates, email click-through rates, conversions from different emails, from different campaigns, the coupon codes you're using–track it all. That way, you can use the data to show you which ones are performing well and which ones are weak. Once you figure that out, you can tweak the inferior campaigns until they perform up to standard.

Ignored Email Real Estate

We all know that emails are great profit centers that should be capitalized on, but there are several emails that all ecom companies send but do not properly use. Most companies neglect these two types of emails out of ignorance; they don't realize that these emails get many times the open rate and click-through rate of any other email they will ever send. That's why I want to bring these emails to your attention now.

Receipt Email

The receipt email gives the customer an overview of their purchase. It has a ridiculously high open rate (in excess of 70 percent on average in my businesses) because people check their receipts. They open it, and they may even file it or print it.

Most email open rates are around 20 percent or less, so an email with a 70 percent open rate means a whole lot more eyeballs are viewing that real estate.[32] It's the perfect place to insert an offer or a coupon to persuade them to purchase again. This can be either a new customer offer or a dynamic offer based on their purchase.

Alternatively, if your shopping cart allows it, you can automatically give them a discount on a related item. Just say in the email, "Did you realize you could also get this? Here's the coupon."

Shipping Notification or Tracking Link Email

Almost every single person opens the shipping notification email. They want to know where their product is and check their tracking number.

Shipping notification emails typically have 80 percent to 90 percent open rates in most businesses—even higher than the receipt email. More people see this email than any other email you send.

Those kinds of open rates make the shipping notification a great place for yet another subtle offer. This could be a dynamic offer based on what they purchased or an offer tied to shipping, such as free shipping for orders over a certain amount. It might not always have the most ridiculous take rate, but an offer in this email still has a higher take rate than nothing at all.

---

[32] (2016). Email Marketing Benchmarks. *Mailchimp Research.*
https://mailchimp.com/resources/research/email-marketing-benchmarks/

Due to so many customers seeing this offer, it's easy to gauge success rates. If it's not working, swap it out with a different offer. If that doesn't work, swap that out with another. Keep doing this until you find something that works, and stick to it. You'll never have another email get as many eyeballs as these do, so it's worth testing till you hit a winner.

Conclusion

To most business owners, the back end doesn't seem nearly as exciting as the front end. But the truth is, if you use back-end marketing correctly, you can outperform all of your competitors who are focusing all their attention on the front end.

By targeting the right segments with the right offers, you can get even more out of the people who already like you. But to make your back end work automatically for you, you have to use what you've learned from the other chapters of the book. Pulling data as discussed in Chapter 7 and using it to better understand the customer life cycles allows for granular segmentation, and many of the advertising techniques applicable to front-end marketing also apply to the back end. Get those in place, and you can do what so many business owners dream about–build a profitable business that grows on autopilot.

Chapter 10 Summary

 Back-end marketing is for existing customers only.

 Study your data to figure out your customers' life cycles and properly segment your customers for advertising.

 Use retargeting promotions to incentivize existing customers to buy more, reenergize declining customers, and revive dormant customers.

 Implement the four core email marketing campaigns: the new customer campaign, the VIP campaign, the win-back campaign, and ignored real estate campaign.

FINAL THOUGHTS

Phew! Brain dump complete.

I know that was a ton of information I just threw at you, and that your head is probably spinning with ideas. You may feel overwhelmed, as this book isn't something I would consider light reading. But that's okay, you can handle it. The subconscious is a magical thing that even now is processing what you've just read and connecting the dots to help you improve your business.

Let this information percolate for a day or two, then come back to this book and re-read the section you feel can make the biggest impact in your business. I've tried to arrange these ideas and strategies in a logical format so you can easily refer back to them as needed.

Quick Win Philosophy

While you should give your brain a little time to digest, the worst thing you can do with what you learned in *Ecommerce Evolved* is sit and think about it for too long. An anonymous but well-known quote that I live by states "More occurs from movement than will ever happen from meditation and contemplation," which basically means, "Take ACTION, ANY ACTION."

We humans build momentum in our lives through action, and the best way I've found to take action in a practical and productive manner is through "Quick Wins." A quick win is something that has an immediate and visible result that can be delivered quickly after being implemented. It does not, however, have to be profound or have long-term impact.

A quick win could be something as simple as adding a PayPal checkout button to your mobile checkout process, turning a multi-page checkout into a single page, or even adding a coupon code to your order receipt email. Each of these by themselves may not seem like much, but the biggest benefit is what happens to YOU with each of these wins. Each win puts a smile on your face, it provides you with proof that your business can improve, it maintains excitement, and it builds momentum to help you effect massive change in your business over time.

So my advice to you right now is this: don't try to paint a Picasso. Start with a few stick figures and smiley faces to get the ball rolling NOW. Let the momentum you build with each quick win lead to your Picasso.

Jump to The Front of the Line

Even though this book is a complete road map to success, there will be people who want to jump to the front of the line and have me personally look over their ideas, start-ups, or existing businesses. In fact, the closer this book got to going to print, the more people came out of the woodwork asking for my help.

I usually only do this for my Black Label Mastermind members because it takes a lot of time, but I decided to break my own rule and help out a few friends. I went through their businesses with a fine-toothed comb and identified the gaps that were preventing growth, helped them plug the leaks that were causing them to lose customers and sales, and suggested some simple improvements that would enable them to scale more profitably. And in every single case we saw immediate and dramatic increases.

I also remembered something as I helped these companies out...I absolutely LOVE tinkering, critiquing, and helping people with their ecommerce businesses, and I want to do more of it. Nothing gets me more excited than helping a business double or triple in size while at the same time automating it to free up more of the owner's time.

I realize, though, that once this book is available to millions the demands on my time will increase and it'll be much harder to accommodate everyone who wants personal help from me and my team. So I've created something special just for the readers of this book. I've opened up some space in our Build Grow Scale Academy so that I can critique your business, talk with you, and help you implement the tweaks and improvements that will take your business to the next level.

 If you are interested in joining the BGS Academy, I'd like to invite you to apply for the program here:

http://www.buildgrowscale.com/academy

After you apply, we'll set up a call to go over your current situation and goals, and to see if the Academy program is a good fit for you and your business. If it is, we could be working together on growing your business in as little as a week.

With that, I will end by saying that this book is your playbook. Don't just read this and then put it up on a shelf to collect dust. Using any one strategy from this book could completely revolutionize your business and your life.

Read It. Use It. Own It.

ABOUT THE AUTHOR

Tanner Larsson is the co-founder of 80/20 Media, an Ecommerce brand incubator, and the CEO of BuildGrowScale.com. He launched his first ecommerce venture from his childhood bedroom in 2001. Since then he has founded or partnered in over a dozen different businesses in markets such as Home Services, Health & Fitness, Guns & Survival, Kitchen Accessories, Supplements & Nutraceuticals, Business Education, and HVAC.

In addition to scaling his own ecom brands (without outside funds), Tanner operates his own fulfillment facility, which packs and ships tens of thousands of products a month. In short, he knows a thing or two about selling physical products online.

Tanner is also the founder and facilitator of an exclusive ecommerce syndicate called Black Label, a mastermind composed of the best and brightest marketers, CEOs, and entrepreneurs in the ecommerce space.

Tanner lives with his wife and two children in Reno, NV. For more information about Tanner, you can check out BuildGrowScale.com or reach out to him on social media at:

Facebook: http://facebook.com/MarketingWithTanner

Twitter: http://twitter.com/buildgrowscale

LinkedIn: https://www.linkedin.com/in/tannerlarsson